# PRAISE FOR
# *NO REGRETS* AND
# PAUL NICCUM

*"Far too many business books fail to address the strong emotional under-current that can dictate whether a business fails or succeeds.* No Regrets *is not filled with theory or conjecture. Every lesson in this book is based on Paul's personal experience—success or failure, example or warning. Paul is an expert at helping business owners grow and maximize the value of their business before there's an offer on the table. Paul knows what he's talking about. Paul is the real deal."*

—**Darren Hardy**, former publisher and founding editor of
*SUCCESS* magazine, *New York Times* best-selling author,
and CEO mentor

*"Paul has the ability to package and present companies to potential acquirers who would never have seen the fit or opportunities they could foster together. Paul knows how to package to market, and the tips he shares in* No Regrets *will be invaluable to any business owners looking to maximize the outcome from their sales."*

—**Marc Sparks**, CEO of Timber Creek Capital
and author of *They Can't Eat You*

*"Paul's ability to connect the dots and tap into his vast network provided us with the resources we needed to grow into a new vertical. Any business owner looking to grow by exploiting new verticals will benefit from reading* No Regrets."

—**Cody Foster,** co-founder of Advisors Excel

"I worked with Paul early on during my exit strategy process. Working with Paul helped provide a road map that allowed me to grow my business, establish my desired exit strategy, and complete my ideal sale. I am still with the company that acquired mine ten years ago. A decade after the sale, and I couldn't be happier with the outcome."

**—Jim Helmer,** former CEO of Advantage Graphics


"Paul used his vision to help us quickly expand our reach into new vertical markets, which accelerated our growth."

**—Mark Rossi**, former Marketing Communication Services president of Merrill Corporation


"Working with Paul has helped bring clarity to the question of how to exit a business. From beginning to end, the 'why, what, won't, when' process for building an exit strategy that Paul shares in No Regrets has provided me with a clear roadmap to build my business in the best possible way now so that I can have the best possible exit later."

**—Misty Lown**, CEO of More Than Just Great Dance and author of Amazon best seller *One Small Yes*


"Working with Paul regarding the accelerated growth and related capital and acquisitions was always proactive and collaborative."

**— Bruce Kennedy**, branch president, Riverwood Bank


"Working with Paul and his team provided me with my ultimate growth strategy, which gave me the ability to transform my business. Paul is creative, caring, and passionate about helping others as evidenced by the fact that in No Regrets, he shares many invaluable tips about growing and selling a business with thousands of entrepreneurs."

**—Eric Douay**, CEO and founder, Fair Merchant Solutions


"I worked with Paul in many of his companies. I experienced first-hand his creative thinking, strategic positioning talents, and client-centric approach to selling companies. I'm thrilled that he's sharing his passions, experience, and expertise in No Regrets."

**—Ann Smallman**, twenty-year business partner

"*I was first a vendor and client of Paul's. Then we became business partners, peers, and friends, a relationship that has lasted for more than twenty-five years. Paul's ability to mentor other business owners is priceless. His knowledge of buying and selling businesses and his creative mind are assets to anyone he works with. He has generously filled* No Regrets *with the lessons he's learned over the years to help other businesses. I can honestly say Paul's can-do attitude and unwavering entrepreneurial spirit was a big part of my decision to pursue my own business.*"

—**Chris Freytag**, founder of Get Healthy U and Get Healthy U TV and author of *Move to Lose, The Two Week Total Body Turnaround,* and *Choose This!* cookbook

"*I worked with Paul for more than fifteen years on many acquisitions and dispositions. I was always amazed at his creativity and his ability to develop deals that were advantageous to both parties. If anyone can help business owners walk away from a sale without regrets, it's Paul Niccum.*"

— **Gerald Hicks**, retired principal with CliftonLarsonAllen, LLP

"*I am a friend of Paul's and have worked for and with him throughout my career. I wholeheartedly believe in Paul's ability to grow, package, and quickly market companies for sale. As valuable as these qualities are, Paul's biggest asset is the way he truly cares for others and what is best for them. Paul wrote* No Regrets *to help people, and any business owners looking to sell who read* No Regrets *will set themselves up for regret-free sales.*"

—**Anthony Nermyr**, former CEO of Outdoor Improvements, former business partner, and friend

"*I was planning to buy a competitor for an all-cash deal. Paul helped me present and close the deal with little cash down. This strategy, which is one of many strategies that Paul shares in* No Regrets, *has become an invaluable part of my growth plans as I work toward my exit goal.*"

—**Chad Tompkins**, president of WTC Engineering

# NO
# REGRETS

# NO
# REGRETS

### How to Grow and Then Exit Your Business, Emotionally and Financially Strong

# Paul Niccum

Vision Lake Publishing

Published by Vision Lake Publishing.

For ordering information or special discounts for bulk purchases, please contact:

Vision Lake Publishing
www.VisionLakePublishing.com

Cover design, composition, and editing by Accelerate Media Partners, LLC

Hardcover ISBN: 978-0-9987646-0-3
EPUB ISBN: 978-0-9987646-1-0
Kindle ISBN: 978-0-9987646-2-7

Library of Congress Control Number: 2017935038

Printed in the United States of America.

# DEDICATION

*To every entrepreneur who has taken the risks involved with starting a company and who has endured the emotional roller coaster required to grow it. You deserve a no-regrets exit.*

# CONTENTS

# FOREWORD

## BY DARREN HARDY,

Former Publisher and Founding Editor of
*SUCCESS* magazine, *New York Times* Best-Selling
Author, and CEO Mentor

**LIKE YOU, I AM AN ENTREPRENEUR.** I've started, grown, and sold numerous businesses. Some of those sales were phenomenal successes. Others could have gone better. Some of those businesses I shouldn't have sold. Some I should have sold at a different time, to a different buyer, for a different price. Of course, you realize these things after the fact when it's too late and regret ensues.

Thankfully, it's not too late for you. Preventing mistakes and regrets begins with awareness and learning from others. My mentor Jim Rohn told me, "You can learn from your mistakes, but it is better to learn from other people's mistakes, and it's best to learn from other people's successes." When it comes to growing and selling a business, *No Regrets* offers each of these opportunities. In *No Regrets*, Paul Niccum takes you through his vast experience of buying and selling businesses. He shows you what to avoid and highlights best practices to follow.

I've spent my life assessing and analyzing some of the world's most successful entrepreneurs. I've had the pleasure to study, interview, and learn how business leaders like Steve Jobs, Elon Musk, Richard Branson, Jeff Bezos, Mark Zuckerberg, and others operate and grow their companies. In addition to learning firsthand how they grow, I also get to see their mistakes. One of the mistakes I have observed is how often most entrepreneurs fail to plan. They fail to plan for growth, they fail to plan for the lifestyle rigors of business ownership, and they fail to plan for the wild emotional roller coaster that is entrepreneurship.

I talked about these failures in my book *The Entrepreneur Roller Coaster*, in which I examined why two-thirds of all small businesses fail.

Overwhelmingly, failure is not due to outside factors such as economics. It's due to an internal factor: emotions. The unexpected and terrifying emotional roller coaster entrepreneurs experience is the greatest factor in why most new business owners quit and ultimately fail. But what about those third who hang on? What about those third who succeed? *No Regrets* is for that third. *No Regrets* shows successful entrepreneurs like you how to grow your business strategically so you can maximize your value and successfully exit your business with no regrets.

The tricky aspect about growing your business is that not all growth is equal. This is particularly true when you're gearing up to sell your business. The strategy and direction of your growth greatly determines what kind of buyer you can court and the valuation they will place on your business. Failing to think about your decisions—failing to weigh the risks and the potential outcomes of your growth strategy—will lead to unintended consequences when you go to sell your business. It will lead to regret.

*No Regrets* artfully outlines how to prepare for the right kind of growth that will result in the best exit strategy for your business. By showing you how to grow your business and how to plan for an exit, Paul makes you more aware of the choices that might lead you *away* from your desired outcome.

By sharing past mistakes and lessons learned, Paul will help you make smarter decisions, so when it comes time to exit your business, you will feel great about the sale. While it may not seem like it now, feeling great about how you exit your business is huge. As entrepreneurs like Paul and I know, making the wrong sale takes an almost indescribable emotional toll on you, your employees, and your customers.

Far too many business books fail to address the strong emotional undercurrent that can dictate whether a business fails or succeeds. Paul's assessment of the emotional aspects of selling a business is spot on. Paul demonstrates exactly how and why selling a business is much more emotionally draining than most entrepreneurs anticipate by sharing the lessons he learned while starting, growing, buying, and selling businesses. He then shows how to avoid these heartaches by planning for growth that will lead to your sale.

*No Regrets* is not filled with theory or conjecture. Every lesson in this book is based on Paul's personal experience—success or failure, example or warning. Paul is an expert at helping business owners grow and maximize the value of their business before there's an offer on the table. Paul knows what he's talking about. Paul is the real deal.

When I worked with Paul at *SUCCESS* magazine, Paul applied his learnings of buying, growing, and selling companies to help *SUCCESS* explode into new growth channels. After our days at *SUCCESS*, Paul continued his growth and development by studying my INSANE PRODUCTIVITY curriculum and attending my High-Performance Forum. Paul is also an alumnus of my private High-Performance ELITE group. Since participating in both, Paul has continued to achieve incredible results and successful business exits! I now use Paul as my model entrepreneur avatar because he epitomizes the top business leaders that adorn the covers of *SUCCESS* magazine. He is a leader with a constant growth mindset, he continually learns and applies his learnings to achieve extraordinary growth, and his results consistently have an outstanding impact in the world.

With *No Regrets* in your hands and Paul as your guide, you now have all it takes to strategically grow your business, develop the perfect exit strategy for you, make your impact, and then gracefully exit feeling prosperous, happy, and soulfully fulfilled.

DARREN HARDY
**Miami Beach, 2017**

# PREFACE

## HOW TO MAKE *NO REGRETS*
## WORK FOR YOU

I wrote *No Regrets* after watching countless business owners struggle to successfully exit their businesses. When you finish reading *No Regrets*, I want you to have the tools you need to successfully sell your business with no regrets.

At the end of each chapter, I've created a journaling section that includes at least three questions for you to answer. The intent of the journal entries is for you to take the lessons you've learned in the corresponding chapter and apply them to your own business. For example, if a chapter discusses developing an exit strategy, at the end of that chapter, the questions prompting your journal entries will help you develop an exit strategy for your own business. If you participate in each journal entry, by the end of *No Regrets*, you will have answered enough questions to get started on the path to a no-regrets sale.

I also recommend highlighting the ideas you want to implement in your own business and adding them to your journal section. Perhaps they're ideas you're not ready to address yet but will want to take a closer look at in the future.

As I discuss throughout the book, I created a similar journal before selling my own businesses and referred to it throughout the sales process. Once your journal is complete, refer to it as you grow and expand your business. Chances are, your plans and desired outcomes for your sale will change. Referring back to your journal entries will help you track, modify, and confirm your changes.

# ACKNOWLEDGMENTS

My life would not be what it is, nor would the journey be so enjoyable and the experience so rich, had I not been fortunate enough to share it with so many wonderful people.

To my wife, Sandi, my soulmate who inspires me, picks me up after each stumble, and cheers me on when I need it most, thank you. I love you with all my heart.

To my kids, Dan, Jen, and Lexi, you give the *why* and *what* to the meaning of my life. Your love and support keeps me going, and I thank God every day for you.

To my parents, Gloria and Roger, Ron and Gladie, and Richard and Leslie, you have always believed in me, guided me through lessons learned, and given me so many unbelievable experiences that I will never forget.

To my sisters, Cindy, Traci, and Sara, I know I can always count on you to be there for me.

To my friends, thank you for all your wise insights, unconditional friendships, and fun-filled adventures.

Lastly, I'd like to thank the professional book publishing team of Reed Bilbray, Ivy Hughes, and Erica Jennings with Accelerate Media Partners for helping me bring this book to life.

# INTRODUCTION

*"Profit by the mistakes of others; you may not live long enough to make them all yourself."*

— FLOYD "NIC" NICCUM

**AT 3:02 A.M. ON JUNE 14, 1999,** I woke up in a cold sweat, looked at my sleeping wife, stared at the ceiling, and thought, "What the hell am I doing?"

In five hours, I would put on my new Joseph Abboud black pinstriped suit, jump into my Jag, and drive from my suburban home to downtown Minneapolis to sign my marketing communications company, Alternatives Communications Group (Alternatives), over to Merrill Corporation. Following that meeting, I would walk into the Alternatives quarterly company meeting at a nearby Radisson Hotel and tell eighty employees who I considered family that I no longer owned the company they'd worked so hard to build.

Thinking about the pending sale made me sick to my stomach, so I got up and wandered aimlessly around the house. I'd started Alternatives in 1990 with a few thousand dollars, a computer, three customers, and two employees. Prior to that, I sold wholesale auto parts for a Minnesota Toyota dealer. That job taught me how to define and find markets versus trying to sell to everyone. In 1983, while working at Toyota and balancing my college course load, I started working for a marketing printing company called Sales Communications Resources (SCR). Two years later, I became a minority owner in SCR.

I started Alternatives after SCR was sold to memorabilia manufacturer Jostens in 1989. I saw a gap in the printing services market and filled it. Before I launched Alternatives, if clients needed multiple printing services, such as catalogs, direct mail, and high-quality marketing brochures, they had to contact multiple manufacturers. Alternatives streamlined that process by representing multiple niche manufacturers. We ensured that our clients had a single contact while protecting their brands across a number of print manufacturing facilities. The result was a one-stop integrated solution for every client's printing needs.

Initially, my first two employees and I operated Alternatives from a Minnetonka, Minnesota, apartment that was next to a prestigious business high-rise called the Carlson Center. This was intentional. The apartment's mailing address was 1 Carlson Place, which gave the appearance that we worked in the high-end neighboring business center that I couldn't afford.

We had a lot of laughs working out of that apartment office. I would show up each morning with my two female coworkers while the other tenants left their apartments for their real offices. We always wondered—and laughed—about what the other tenants must have thought we were doing all day. I'm not sure what they thought we were up to, but we spent most of the day working out of the living room and using the single bedroom as a conference room.

We stayed in that apartment and hustled for two years before expanding into an industrial park. As we grew, we took on more space, added more employees, and developed stronger emotional connections to each other. Before I knew it, nine years had passed, and Alternatives had acquired a few companies and grown to $25 million a year in revenue.

On that morning of June 14, 1999, I walked down the stairs of my house like Gordon Gecko, the king of "greed is good" from the movie *Wall Street*. That isn't me at all. The problem was that I was about to make one of the biggest errors business owners make: I was about to sell my business long before I was ready, simply because I couldn't resist the financial offer. For a moment, this temptation made me someone I wasn't. As many sellers have experienced, getting an offer from someone who wants to buy something you've built from the ground up is a *huge* ego boost. It can make you feel like Gordon, but the feeling is fleeting.

As soon as I saw my kids eating breakfast and getting ready for school, I returned to reality and focused on my family. They asked me to join them. The last thing I wanted was food, but I sat and ate a piece of dry toast. As my kids talked about their days my mind wandered to happier times, drifting from the pending sale to many great memories of the startup phase of Alternatives.

Getting into my Jag to drive to the closing in downtown Minneapolis, all I could think about was that apartment and my two founding employees—both of whom were still with me. I knew their families and they knew mine. They'd been integral to growing Alternatives and developing our culture, which was very family oriented. If our employees needed two hours off in the middle of the day to take their kids to the dentist, we didn't question it. Many of our employees were lifelong friends. Some had even met at Alternatives and then married. What would they think about the sale? What would happen to them and their families? Would they feel betrayed? Although I'd convinced myself that nothing would change for my employees post-sale, I really had no idea what would happen once I sold and was no longer the owner.

The twenty-minute drive to Minneapolis felt like two hours. It was torture because I couldn't get my mind to settle down. The question, "*WHY* am I selling?" was a broken record. Just a few days before, one of my employees had asked if something was going on with Alternatives internally. We had made many previous announcements regarding acquisitions or added services, but he noticed I was being quieter than usual and was visibly nervous. Some odd things had been occurring as well. My wife, Sandi, who didn't come to the office that often, had been making frequent visits to use the copy machine. I needed to keep the sale confidential. Confidentiality is an important element of any merger and acquisition, but in this case, we were selling to a public company, so confidentiality was critical. I didn't want to lie to my employee, so I said, "Something good is going to happen. I just can't tell you what it is yet."

He said, "I sure hope so because I don't know how things could get much better."

I thought about that conversation all the way into the city. Truth be told, I'd never *started out* to sell Alternatives. I wanted to spend time with my new wife and young family and thought the way to do it was by bringing on a financial partner. I didn't *think* about selling until I visited an investment banker who worked in the office park next to Alternatives. He had helped another business obtain financing and had recently sold a business in the same industry as Alternatives, so I went to him looking for a financial partner that could help us grow. The banker talked to a few people and, before I knew it, I had a letter of intent (LOI) from Merrill Corporation, which wanted to buy 100 percent of Alternatives. This was appealing because it meant Alternatives would become part of a successful international public company. I also thought the proposed deal would offer growth opportunities for our clients and long-term security for my employees.

From there, everything was a complete whirlwind, and I made mistake after mistake. Specifically, I didn't have an honest conversation with myself about *WHAT* I wanted from the sale of Alternatives. I didn't develop any sort of plan for the sale, and I never thought about what an exit strategy might look like. I only thought about two things: one, what Merrill would pay and two, what the new opportunities for my clients and employees would look like. I didn't realize that my failure to plan the sale of the company I had put so much emotion and hard work into would take such an emotional toll on me, my employees, my clients, and the buyer.

When I agreed to the sale, I thought about the check that would be wired to me. I also thought about the fact that I was thirty-eight years old and that once I sold Alternatives, I would have the financial freedom to do whatever I wanted. As soon as I walked into the conference room of the Minneapolis high-rise where the closing was held and faced the large team of attorneys, I was no longer interested in the money. I was totally unprepared for what was about to happen.

The spring sun, which shone through the floor-length windows of the building's forty-second floor, blinded me as the lawyers shuffled around what seemed like a ream of paper to sign. I was a complete wreck. I was terrified that I'd just made the worst decision possible for myself, my employees, and my customers. Instead of feeling free, I felt nothing but fear, insecurity, and sadness. Although I continued feeling some negative emotions long after the sale, those emotions paled in comparison to the regret I felt after the closing.

For a business owner, regret is a difficult emotion to manage. Regret is defined as a sad or disappointed feeling brought on by something that has been done and is often triggered by *missed opportunities*. I missed opportunities for Alternatives by selling without thinking through the sale and, once I sold Alternatives, I couldn't get it back, which led to additional regrets.

Selling a business isn't like selling a car. You can't just turn around, sell it, and buy another just like it. When you sell your business and then change your mind about selling it, getting it back is really difficult. So, when you sell without thinking through why you're selling, what you hope to get from the sale, or what you'll do after the sale, you miss opportunities *and* take action that can't be undone.

# re · gret /rə-'gret/

1. feel sad, repentant, or disappointed over (something that has happened or been done, especially a loss or missed opportunity).

Unfortunately, the way I felt when I sold Alternatives is exactly how thousands of other business owners feel when they sell their privately held companies. Why? Because they sell before they are prepared to sell. As I moved through the stages of growing Alternatives, I never thought about what it would be like to *sell* a business. Not just the nuts and bolts of the deal, but the emotional ramifications of selling something I loved that was run by people I cared about. It's impossible to explain the river of emotion that flows when you let go of something that you've built with your own hands. Most business owners are so focused on building their businesses that they don't think about selling it until the sale is over. This is why so many business owners walk away from a sale carrying a basket full of regrets. I know I did.

Emotionally and physically, the time I spent working for the buyer after selling Alternatives was not at all what I envisioned, and it caused a great deal of stress. I didn't like going into the office, couldn't wait to leave the office, and suffered intense, consistent migraines, something I'd never experienced before. The business decisions were no longer mine to make; before the sale, I failed to plan or discuss certain decisions and so I disagreed with some decisions that were being made. I struggled to watch how those decisions negatively affected my customers and employees. Even though I was contracted to stay on five years following the sale, I left before the first year was up. Sadly, during that time, I watched a company that I built from the ground up lose employees, clients, and revenue.

If you want to know what it feels like to sell a privately held business, condense all the emotional highs and lows you've felt while building that business into a single event. If managed ineffectively, these emotions can affect your end results. To help manage these emotions, you have to understand and prepare for what's ahead. As the old saying goes, average people learn from their own mistakes; brilliant people learn from the mistakes and successful learnings of others.

I have built six companies from the ground up, acquired eight privately held businesses, and sold several businesses to public *Fortune 100* and *Fortune 500* companies. Today, through my advisory company, Paradise Capital, I work with business owners to develop plans that will allow them not only to maximize their sale, but also to leave them feeling great about the sale. I can say from experience that the only way to feel great about a sale is to prepare for it. I didn't feel good about a sale until 2015, when I sold the marketing services portion of a company I co-owned called Range, Inc. So, that's sixteen years between the sale of Alternatives and Range, or nearly two decades of buying and selling businesses, before I really understood what I needed to do to feel great about a sale.

With *No Regrets,* I want to help you
prepare for the sale of your business so
you don't end up selling to the wrong
buyer, for the wrong reasons, for the
wrong amount, at the wrong time.

With *No Regrets*, I want to help you prepare for the sale of your business so you don't end up selling to the wrong buyer, for the wrong reasons, for the wrong amount, at the wrong time. I'll do this by explaining the steps to closing a regret-free sale. First, I'll walk you through the presale process, which is best done well before you plan to market and sell your business. This presale process allows you to clearly define and build out both your exit strategy and your growth strategy. Then, we'll talk emotions and why it's so important to consider how the sale will affect you, your employees, and clients *before* you sell. We'll address valuations, how packaging affects marketing, the sales process, what to expect at closing, life after the sale, and finally, how each of these components will allow you to walk away with no regrets.

Throughout *No Regrets*, I will contrast my worst sale—the Alternatives sale—with my best sale—the Range sale—so you can see what it means to feel good about a sale and what it means to leave one with regrets.

If there's one thing I learned about selling a business the wrong way, it's that my hindsight can help others. As both a buyer and a seller, my mission is to help all sellers complete a sale that leaves no regrets. I want to save you from the mistakes I made by giving you the tools to successfully prepare for and navigate a sale. *No Regrets* will show you how to sell a business without sacrificing the well-being of your employees, your customers, yourself, and your family. At the end of each chapter, I will list key questions to ask yourself as you prepare for your sale. By the end of *No Regrets*, you will have twenty-two journal entries that will help prepare you for your no-regrets exit.

If there's one thing you need to know about selling a business, it's that the only sale you'll truly enjoy is the one that leaves no regrets. When you look back on your sale in five, ten, or fifteen years, I want you to feel great about it. I want you to say, "I'm so glad I did that," not, "I wish I would have asked for this outcome, thought about my employees, or kept my business." Let's start planning for a sale that leaves you with no regrets.

**Paul Niccum**

# SECTION 1

# PREPARE TO SELL YOUR BUSINESS

# CHAPTER 1

➡

# BUILD AN EXIT

# STRATEGY

*"The meeting of preparation with opportunity
generates the offspring we call luck."*

— TONY ROBBINS

**RIGHT AFTER I SIGNED ALTERNATIVES OVER** to Merrill, I pulled my Jag to the side of the road and threw up. As I said in the introduction, going into the sale on that June day, I knew it wasn't right. I wasn't ready to get out of the business, and it was too late to do anything about it. Years later, I understood that the reason I ended up selling before I was ready was that I'd never asked myself, "Paul, why are you doing this?"

As a business owner, know that at some point you will have to exit your business. You'll either shut it down and liquidate, pass away, transfer ownership of it to family or partners, or sell it. If selling is how you plan to exit, you must have an exit strategy. If you don't have an exit strategy, you may find yourself on the side of the road throwing up after the sale like I did after closing on my sale of Alternatives.

## WHAT IS AN EXIT STRATEGY?

An exit strategy is your business road map. It's the route that will lead you to exiting your business without regrets.

Specifically, an exit strategy keeps owners free from emotional regrets while transitioning out of their business by:

1. Keeping those who are not ready to sell from selling or jumping at the first offer.

2. Providing a growth compass and personal/business credo.

3. Providing sellers with strong negotiation points based on their why, what, when, and won't, which will be discussed in a moment.

An exit strategy prepares you to react to buyers in a way that puts your company in the best position to reward your efforts, optimizes the best situation for your sale, and helps you develop a sale that has no regrets.

---

## Selling a business without an exit strategy is like running a marathon without a finish line.

---

Your exit strategy will also prevent you from making major mistakes by walking through the uncertainties of a sale before they happen. For example:

→ What if you're preparing to sell and an acquisition opportunity arises?

→ Would an acquisition net a larger sale in the future, or would it be a temporary distraction?

→ What if you end up needing to sell sooner than you anticipated due to a health issue? What does your succession plan look like?

Whatever the uncertainty, if you develop an exit strategy before it arises, you will save yourself the heartache of making a quick decision that doesn't follow the outcome you planned for.

Selling a business without an exit strategy is like running a marathon without a finish line. Without one, you'll never know where you're headed.

## FOLLOW YOUR BLUEPRINTS TO THE PERFECT SALE

Following an exit strategy for your business is like following a set of blueprints while building a house—it helps you navigate each stage of the sale. It also ensures that you stop and check your progress at the right time so you achieve your desired outcome.

If you're building a house, you might take a look at your blueprints before there's a shovel in the ground and realize that you don't have the budget for the design you wanted. Maybe that means you put the project on hold. Maybe the opposite happens when you look at the blueprints. Maybe you realize you *have* the budget so you move forward by signing contracts. The point is, blueprints help you decide when and if it's time to move ahead with construction or a sale.

## BUILDING WITHOUT BLUEPRINTS

Without blueprints, you may look at the foundation after it's laid and realize it takes up the *entire* lot. So much for that three-car garage you wanted. Or maybe when the whole house is finished, you find yourself looking at a one-bedroom Tudor when you wanted a three-bedroom contemporary design. In either scenario, you end up with something you regret because you didn't *plan* your outcome. If you don't have a plan, you'll never get what you want. The same concept applies to selling a business.

---

Do not sell a business you love before
thinking about the consequences.

---

Many sellers who *think* they want to sell develop an exit strategy, look at it, and think, "I actually don't want to sell. I'm not ready." Like the homeowner who wasn't ready to build, these sellers delay the process. Maybe they realize they love the industry they're in but want to change their position within it. Maybe instead of selling, they realize they need to grow and acquire another company or bring on a new employee or partner.

If I really knew what I was getting before I sold Alternatives, I wouldn't have sold. I certainly wouldn't have been sick on the side of the road immediately after the sale. The point is, do not sell a business you love before thinking about the consequences.

## DEVELOP YOUR WHY, WHAT, WHEN AND WON'T

An exit strategy does not tell you *how* to sell your business. It tells you *why* you're selling, *what* elements of the sale are negotiable, *when* you plan to sell, and which elements of the sale you *won't* negotiate on.

To help my clients develop an exit strategy, I first get them to establish their why, what, when, and won't by having them answer a few questions. Your why, what, when, and won't may change over time. Each one can affect the other so it's important that you journal, track, adjust, and confirm that you're okay with each change you make along the way.

Let's use your health to show how pieces of your why, what, when, and won't may change. Say you establish a why, what, when, and won't that you're comfortable with. You're happy with your strategy and use it to grow your company. However, say one day you find out that you're sick. Suddenly, instead of wanting to wait five years to sell your business as you had planned, you want to sell it within the year so you can focus on your health. In this case, your *when* changes. This scenario might also change your what, won't, or why as well.

In another scenario, say you're happy with your why, what, when, and won't, but someone approaches you out of the blue about selling your business for five times your desired amount. Suddenly, your *why* changes because the new offer will allow you to do something you've never dreamed of. These examples demonstrate how your why, what, when, and won't can impact each other as well as the sale of your business.

*Why* questions explain your motivation behind the sale; *what* questions help determine the deal structure and selling price; *when* questions are all about timing; and *won't* questions provide the negotiating tools.

---

## DEFINING YOUR "EXIT STRATEGY"

**WHY** are you selling?

**WHAT** is negotiable?

**WHEN** are you selling?

Which elements **WON'T** you negotiate on?

---

## WHY QUESTIONS:

→ Why do I want to sell?

→ Why do I want the additional proceeds?

→ Why is this the right time for me to sell?

→ Why do I want to do something different?

→ Why would someone want my company?

## WHAT QUESTIONS:

→ What is my company worth?

→ What price would I like to get for my company and how is that different than what it's currently worth?

→ What do I need to do today to increase the value of my company so I can sell in $x$ years?

→ What does my ideal buyer look like?

→ What do I want to do after the sale *or* what role would I like to take within the company after the sale?

→ What key staff do I want in place post-sale?

## WHEN QUESTIONS:

→ When is my company going to be worth the most?

→ When is the right time to begin the sales process?

→ When do I want to retire?

→ When will a sale be right for my employees?

→ When will a sale be best for my customers?

## WON'T QUESTIONS:

→ What type of buyer won't I sell to?

→ What won't I negotiate on in terms of moving the location of the company?

→ What type of sale won't I take?

→ What won't I allow to happen to my clients and key employees?

→ What about our quality of what we stand for won't I allow the buyer to change?

That first question in the bunch—*why* do I want to sell?—is the most important and should be viewed as your personal vision statement. The reason most sellers *think* they want to sell and the *actual* motivation behind the sale could be miles apart. At this point, you must assess your personal value beyond the business. You must separate your personal goals from your business goals, which have likely been intertwined while you've been building your business.

## ASK THE RIGHT QUESTIONS AND AVOID THESE THREE MISTAKES

Typically, when sellers don't understand *why* they want to sell, one of three things happens. One, as soon as the seller's noncompete expires, he or she starts a new business that's nearly identical to the one sold. Not only is the seller competing with the buyer, but the seller often ends up taking some of the buyer's employees. This isn't fair to the buyer and leaves the seller with emotional regrets. It tugs at their integrity and creates a multitude of headaches because the seller is essentially rebuilding what they just sold. There's no point in going through the hardship of selling one business and starting a similar one years later when you could have kept and grown the original business.

Two, the seller starts a business in an unrelated field on a whim and ends up losing a lot of money. This scenario occurs when sellers don't fully understand *why* they want to sell and decide to keep working after the sale without defining what working means. This is the car dealer who sells his or her dealership and decides to open a Thai restaurant. Just because he or she had a great dinner doesn't mean they have the necessary experience in restaurant management to start a restaurant. In this case, the dealer wants to keep working, but has no idea what that means so he or she dives into something that might not work.

Three, the seller stays on with the new company and either quits or experiences a painful transition into the buyer's company. I'll talk about how this happened when I sold Alternatives later.

## ASK THE RIGHT QUESTIONS, CLOSE THE RIGHT DEAL

The answers to your *what* questions will help match what you hope to get from the sale financially with what a buyer will realistically pay.

The answers to your *won't* questions are your non-negotiables. They pertain to what you want for your employees and yourself following the sale. If I had answered my wont's—the things I would *not* negotiate on—before selling Alternatives, I never would have sold when I did.

The answers to your *when* questions will determine whether you need to wait to sell, grow, acquire another company, find ways to differentiate within your market, or introduce new systems that will be more attractive to sellers *before* you go to market.

Because I've bought and sold numerous businesses and helped others do the same, it's easy to understand how sellers who do not first understand their why, what, when, and won't end up walking into a sale they end up regretting. Every seller gets excited by the possibility of a sale. It's enormously gratifying to know someone else wants to buy something you've built from the ground up. But once that feeling disappears, sellers who haven't thought about the future typically become bored, suffer emotional consequences, or regret the decision to sell altogether. Sellers who use their why, what, when, and won't as their growth compass or personal/business credo rarely sell a business before they're ready.

## CHOOSE A BASELINE VALUATION

While you're working through your exit strategy, choose a valuation method that will help determine what your company is worth. This baseline valuation will measure the value of your company year over year, allowing you to see what you need to do or adjust year after year to sell your company for a price that will meet your financial and exit strategy goals.

Setting a baseline valuation allows you to plan for and fix *today* so you get the best outcome *tomorrow*.

I will go into further detail about valuations in Chapter 4; however, I would suggest using the standard EBITDA (earnings before interest, taxes, depreciation, and amortization) valuation as your baseline. EBITDA simply factors in your annual income/earnings and adds back expenses, including interest paid, taxes, depreciation, and amortization expenses.

When it is time to market your business, you and a group of advisors will build an adjusted EBITDA model, adding back other expenses taken, as well as look at other models based on type of business and how specific buyers will value your business. I will show you how to calculate EBITDA and will address the different variables and other ways to value your business. It is up to you and your A-Team, who we will also discuss in Chapter 4, to advise how to position your company in such a way that you get the best overall value that also matches your exit goals.

## CREATE A PLAN A AND PLAN B

The sooner you develop your why, what, when, and won't, the sooner you can develop a Plan A and a Plan B for the sale. Your Plan A is what you desire from the sale. It's your Holy Grail, your best-case scenario, your pie-in-the-sky outcome, your win-win situation. Of course, Plan A rarely happens.

Your Plan B is a more realistic look at what might happen and is much more likely to occur than Plan A. Your Plan B addresses some what-ifs such as:

→ What if you find a buyer that will keep key staff but move the physical location of the company?

→ What if you look for a private buyer, but are approached by a public one?

Your Plan B walks through some of those uncertainties we talked about earlier so you're prepared to handle them when they come up.

## NO EXIT STRATEGY? NO PLANS? LOTS OF REGRETS

As I've reflected on my experience with the Alternatives sale, I've realized that I had actually been indirectly involved with the sale of a business years before. That sale also led to regrets.

In 1983, I got a job working for Sales Communications Resources (SCR). By 1985, thanks to some innovations I made, my boss sold me 20 percent of SCR for a whopping $1 and my signature on a one-year noncompete. So, I received ownership in SCR without any debt and gained a new silver Mercedes, access to a nearby country club, and use of the company boat.

One day, my partner approached me about selling SCR. I was young. I found the possibility of a sale exciting and thought it might give me some extra cash. I did not think about what else I might want to do with my career or how the sale would affect my clients or other employees. I was too focused on doing what I did well, which was selling marketing services, to really think about what selling SCR would mean beyond getting some extra money.

## IF YOU DON'T KNOW WHY, WHAT, AND WON'T, FORGET ABOUT WHEN

It turns out that my partner wasn't thinking too much about what the sale of SCR would mean either. Like so many business owners, he didn't have an exit strategy. He *thought* he wanted to get out of the business—it was volatile and capital intense—but as far as I knew, he never really had a heart-to-heart with himself about *why* he wanted to leave. Therefore, he made two of the most common mistakes sellers who don't really want to sell make. They are:

→ Staying and working with the new company without knowing what that means or what the motivations are for staying.

→ Starting a business in an unrelated industry without a plan because the seller misses running a business.

When Jostens, which is a memorabilia manufacturer, bought SCR, my former partner left after six months. It was too difficult for him to accept the decisions made by the new leadership, which isn't uncommon following a sale, so he exited.

After my partner left Jostens, he decided to continue working without thinking about what that meant. As a result, he bought—and in short order, closed—a franchise in an unrelated field and lost most of his proceeds from the SCR sale. This happens a lot, too. Owners go into industries they're unfamiliar with following a sale simply because they can't sit still.

Approaching the SCR sale, my partner wasn't ready to quit working. He also wasn't ready to leave the commercial printing industry. In fact, he wasn't really ready to sell at all. Since he didn't understand *why* he wanted to sell his business or *when* he really wanted to sell it, he ended up leaving with regrets. This was a mistake I made ten years later when I sold Alternatives.

## IF YOU DON'T KNOW WHAT AND WON'T

I can't tell you how many business owners who fail to address their what and won't end up taking the first offer to cross their desk. The SCR sale is a perfect example.[1] Negotiations for the SCR sale started at a country club when one of my partner's friends approached him about selling SCR to Jostens. On the surface, that first offer from Jostens seemed ideal, but first offers are very rarely the best option for the seller, their employees, and the company.

Jostens sold yearbooks to colleges and SCR sold recruiting materials to colleges. At the time of the sale, Jostens was interested in expanding its yearbook printing plant production and wanted to augment yearbook production with commercial print work, which is what SCR did. Similar industry, great offer, no brainer, right? Well, that's what my partner thought, but because he jumped at the first offer, he missed the opportunity to make more money, which was his third mistake.

If my partner had planned his exit, he could have continued building SCR until it was better positioned within the market and potentially made more money on the sale. He could have made SCR more attractive to other yearbook companies such as Life Touch Studios and Taylor Corp., which were two other local companies in the same market, prompting those companies to competitively bid on SCR.

## NO REGRETS TIP

Don't jump at the first offer. They are rarely the best option for the seller, their employees, and the company.

---

1   It should be noted here that the events of the SCR sale are from my view point only as a minority owner.

## IF YOU DON'T HAVE A PLAN A OR B

Not only did the SCR sale *not* have an exit strategy, it didn't have a Plan B.

The only plan my partner and I had for the sale followed Jostens' original Plan A for the sale. Jostens had the SCR sales team focus on developing college markets. Great idea—colleges print a lot of marketing materials—but it didn't work. Unfortunately, Jostens was used to yearbook deadlines, which are seasonal. Deadlines for college marketing materials are often unpredictable and occur consistently throughout the year. Before we knew it, we were missing deadlines and losing clients.

As a result, Jostens decided to close the SCR plant. Had we gone into the sale with a Plan B, we could have kept that plant open. We could have outlined how to get 100 or so yearbook sales while also selling the services SCR already sold. This could have had a much better financial and emotional outcome for Jostens and SCR employees.

Had we developed a Plan B for the SCR sale, we also could have developed a realistic, clear strategy regarding what would happen to SCR employees and owners when SCR became a part of Jostens. When the deal came to us, we never thought about how SCR's fifty employees would realistically fit into Jostens' 5,000-employee strong business model. We hoped the transition would be a smooth one, but we didn't have a plan for making that happen. As a result, SCR employees were never really integrated into Jostens. They worked at Jostens, but were this sort of outlying arm that Jostens didn't know what to do with. As a result, many SCR employees left, which left many customer contracts unfulfilled.

Because my partner hadn't really thought about his new role within Jostens, he ended up hating his position and, as I mentioned earlier, left after only six months. With contracts left unfulfilled, a disgruntled staff, and a high staff turnover rate, within two years Jostens ended up divesting what was left of SCR. SCR was a good company and it was heartbreaking to see how selling it negatively affected my partner, who is a very ethical class act gentleman.

Establishing an exit strategy based on your why, what, when, and won't that also includes a Plan A and a Plan B may seem simple, but business owners who fail to do this risk walking away from their sale with intense emotional regrets. This happens because there's a psychological element to selling a business that can cloud your judgment during presale planning. It's incredibly flattering to know that you've found a way to exploit a market and done it so well that someone else wants to pay you for it. But just because you've mastered that market doesn't mean that you know how to *sell* your business. Building a business is completely different than selling one. Your exit strategy provides a road map for both.

---

## Building a business is completely different than selling one. Your exit strategy provides a road map for both.

---

## STAY ON TOP OF YOUR EXIT STRATEGY

To get the most value out of your exit strategy, plan it early and review it and your baseline valuation method often. I review my exit strategies semi-annually to see if they remain valid. Whenever I think of selling, I look at my exit strategy and ask myself three crucial questions that ensure I will not walk into a sale that will leave me filled with regrets. They are:

1. Is the sale right for my customers?
2. Is the sale right for company growth and for my employees?
3. Is the sale right for me?

### Is It Right for My Customers?

A sale that's good for your customers will be good for company growth, provide opportunities for your employees, increase the value of your company, and also benefit you. Asking, "Is this sale right for my customers?" helps determine the driving force behind selling your business *today*.

Answering this question will keep you from selling based on short-term issues such as having a bad year, losing a major account, or watching a new competitor enter the market. None of these are good reasons to sell *today*. They are problems with solutions, not true motivations for selling. Maybe you need to find a new client, change your marketing strategies, offer clients a new service, or start recruiting new sales representatives.

Acknowledging the reason you want to sell today is critical. If your reason is related to something that can be fixed today but you don't recognize or fix that something, you may sell too early, sell before you're ready, or walk away with a whole host of regrets.

### Is It Right for My Company and My Employees?

When you think about whether the sale is right for your company, think about where your company is in terms of market relevance. Is the market or your offering stagnant or in a declining position? Are you going through a strong rebuilding year? Are you experiencing a huge growth curve? Is cash flow causing concerns? Is your company at the top of its growth, or has it peaked or is it just starting to decline? Answering these questions will help determine whether your reasons for selling are valid or situational.

Being stagnant isn't a reason to sell, and it certainly isn't a reason for a buyer to buy. Stagnant companies can affect staff morale and give employees the idea that the company isn't going anywhere. Energy can be created within a declining company as long as it has a growth plan. A stagnant company will not have a growth plan. Even if you think being stagnant is a good reason to leave, you will struggle to find a buyer without a growth plan.

In this case, maybe instead of selling you need a financial partner. Maybe you need to make another adjustment that doesn't involve selling to meet your goals, so that when you do want to sell, a buyer will want to buy.

### Is It Right for Me?

I look at selling a company much like I look at investing in the market. I always wonder, "How much of a return is enough? What gain would I be happy with? What would be a fair deal for the buyer?"

Every time I review my exit strategy, I review it against personal risk versus personal reward. This helps me decide whether to continue with the sales process. I always ask myself, "Would I hold on to or invest in this company?" If the answer is, "Yes, I'd buy this company for that price," or "Yes, I would invest in this company," then I will revisit my why, what, when, and won't. If your why is that you want to retire and relax, then it might be time to sell. If you would invest and your why is that you still love what you're doing, it isn't time to sell.

After I answer these questions, I rank them in order of importance. For me, this final question—is it right for me?—always ranks above the other two. I believe you can have the worst market conditions possible, but if your why is strong enough, that alone is enough to sell. You control your why. You don't control the market.

# ➡ NO REGRETS
# JOURNAL ENTRY

**START YOUR EXIT STRATEGY NOW.** Don't wait until someone approaches you about selling and it's too late. Journal your why, what, when, and won't below.

_____

_____

_____

_____

_____

_____

**COMPLETE YOUR BASELINE VALUATION AND COMPILE A LIST OF KEY PERFORMANCE INDICATORS (KPIs).** What do you need to track as part of your exit journey so, going forward, you can track your results/progress to see where you need to make adjustments?

_____

_____

_____

_____

_____

_____

_____

**LIST WHAT YOU ARE DOING WELL TODAY.** What do clients appreciate most about working with your company? What else can you do for them? Writing this list will help you avoid a knee-jerk reaction (selling too early) to short-term challenges.

_____

_____

_____

_____

_____

_____

_____

_____

_____

_____

_____

_____

_____

_____

**For a free downloadable exit strategy questionnaire, visit www.paradisecapital.biz**

# CHAPTER 2

➡

# DEVELOP A GROWTH STRATEGY

*"Growth is never by mere chance; it is the result of forces working together."*

— JAMES CASH PENNEY

**WHEN I WORK WITH BUSINESS OWNERS** who think they are ready to sell, in addition to their exit strategies, I also ask to see their growth plans. It's important to know if they've executed and achieved their goals, or if they have more to do before they sell. Sometimes, owners who lack a growth plan decide to sell when sales stagnate and they're burned out. They mistakenly believe this is a reason to exit when, in fact, owners who sell before they achieve their ultimate goals often leave the sale with regrets.

To net the best results for your sale and to make sure you don't leave with regrets, develop a growth strategy. Buyers want to see there is an upside, and the seller wants to go out with momentum, knowing they have done all they wanted.

## WHY YOU NEED A GROWTH STRATEGY

You need a growth strategy for two reasons. One, it can provide a plan to fill the gap from your current value to your desired value. Two, it can lead to a no-regrets sale that meets your goals.

### Fill the Gap for Sellers

Once you develop your exit strategy, you may realize that there's a gap between what your company is currently worth and what you'd like to sell it for. Your growth strategy can help fill that gap.

For example, one of my clients who owned a fitness center for youths had a current valuation of $5 million, but wanted to sell her business for $20 million. This left a $15 million gap between what my client wanted and what a buyer would likely pay. To fill that gap, my client needed a plan to grow the company first and find additional synergies that would allow her to expand.

I helped this client build a growth plan. After looking at her current clients—fitness members and the value they provided—we found an underserved adjacent market with similar needs: gymnastics students. We discovered that several gymnastics students were looking for training like the training my client offered.

By adjusting her marketing plan, repackaging her services, and expanding into the fitness and the gymnastics markets, my client was able to grow faster in the same region using the same staff. This helped her fill the gap between what she wanted and what a seller would likely pay.

### It Can Lead to a No-Regrets Sale

Without a growth plan, you may not know if you're going the right direction or how to change directions to get what you want from the sale. A growth plan allows you to track and measure your progress so you don't get burned out when sales decline, go down a path that leaves you without growth, or go down a path that is not as marketable or attractive to buyers, resulting in a smaller return upon your exit. If you don't have a growth plan, you'll never know what you're getting, where you're getting it, or where your business is going. If you don't *plan* your outcome, you may *regret* your outcome.

---

If you don't *plan* your outcome,
you may *regret* your outcome.

---

Many sellers who *think* they want to sell develop an exit strategy, build a growth plan, and then think, "I actually don't want to sell. I'm not ready; maybe I can grow it faster now with a focused plan." They realize they love the industry they're in.

Sometimes, after building a growth plan, these sellers are more energized and want to grow and *then* look to acquire another company or bring on a new employee or partner so they can focus on their strengths and focus on the areas of the business they love. They decide *not* to sell now, but to wait and grow first.

## WHAT COULD HAVE BEEN

If we had developed a growth plan for SCR, we could have expanded its product/service offerings *before* the sale and had a better outcome. For example, we also worked with real estate agents who wore branded shirts and bought other logoed accessories to advertise their brands. If we had developed a growth plan to guide us, we could have expanded our search of buyers to include marketing companies that sold ad specialties or apparel. We could have also looked at signage companies or property photographers as partners. Both options could have resulted in adding more value and selling more products to our existing client base.

If we'd first developed a growth strategy, we would have asked ourselves:

→ What other product offering would agents need that we could sell to them?

→ How could we make the agents' user experience with SCR and the buyer better?

→ Would a sign company that sells front yard signs to agents need design and print services to market properties?

Based on the above questions *we may* have considered selling signs to real estate companies to grow faster.

## FOUR STEPS TO DEVELOP A GROWTH PLAN

When I bought Range, we needed a growth plan. The company had not grown for several years and had actually been experiencing a sales decline. I knew what I wanted and had an exit strategy but needed to revisit how the company went to market so we could start growing. Using the four simple steps outlined below, I built a growth plan that delivered my exit goals after only three years. It also doubled our revenue, achieving a forty-eight-year sales high.

### Step 1: Identify a Market

The first thing I looked at when developing a growth plan for Range was our current client base. I wanted to see if we sold services to any similar businesses. I looked at the products and services that each of our customers bought and asked, "Are they the same? If so, how are they the same? Do we work with companies that are competitors or possible partners that happen to work in the same industry? How do they market? How do they use our products and services?"

I asked these questions because I wanted to know if we could offer the same products to any adjacent markets—adjacent markets being clients that look similar to your existing clients. I did this to become stronger in the markets we already served while also giving us the opportunity to find new markets where we could offer what we already offered to existing clients.

After asking these questions, I thought about what I *should have been* offering in addition to what we already offered.

To expand your list of potential clients, ask yourself, "What else might my current clients buy and who else needs the same services?" Here are some questions to jumpstart this process:

- How many customers do I have that are in the same industry or market?
- What do they currently buy from my company?
- Can I sell the same types of products and services to all of them?
- Are there other adjacent markets that need the same types of offerings?
- What do my clients need that I don't produce now?

You can get this data by sending a survey to key customers or by asking them what other services they would like to see you offer. You can also suggest a new product and ask if your current clients might be interested in it.

When you have a group of similar clients, you can market yourself as an industry expert instead of a generalist. This places you in a leadership position versus a position of jack of all trades, master of none.

It can provide the potential for you to sell more products to the same customers faster. When you become an industry expert, it's much easier to attend trade shows or other industry-specific events not only to learn more, but also to directly target your prospects who will attend and be easier to meet. This is like fishing in a barrel: you know the type of fish that are in the barrel and you know what type of bait they like. All you have to do is drop a line.

Once you establish yourself as an industry expert, you'll generate referrals not only from clients, but also from other partners who want access to your clients. Expanding markets and doing more of what you already do within specific industries will make you more attractive to prospective buyers when you're ready to sell.

Once you establish a market, look at what other market or client type is adjacent to your current clients or the products you already sell.

### Step 2: Establish Market Size

After I identify a market to pursue, I establish the market size: how big is the prospect base, and is the energy to market worth the return? This allows you to monitor your progress in terms of market penetration. Today, you may have 2 percent of the market for your offering and could set a goal to achieve 15 percent over a certain period. Do this by examining what your current clients spend for your products and using that to establish metrics. For example, say hospitals buy your products. If they buy your products for each room they have, you can determine their annual spend ($500,000) by calculating how many rooms (100) they have and then dividing their annual spend (100 divided by $500,000 = $5,000 per room) for an average room spend. Now, find a prospect list through an association or list broker that gives you all the hospitals in your region, along with each hospital's room count. Take your current average room spend, and multiply it by each hospital room count. Do this for each hospital, total them, and you've got a grand total for what your total available market looks like.

### Step 3: Define Your Value Differentiators

You have a defined market and confirmed the market size is large enough to be worth your efforts. Start Step 3 by looking at your internal staff, clients, and competitors. Who else is in your market? What do they do better than you do? How can you compete? Essentially, this begins with your SWOT (strengths, weaknesses, opportunities, and threats) analysis.

See pages 34–36 for an example of a SWOT analysis I use that highlights the opportunities/actions needed for growth. Fill out each section to analyze internal and external factors. Each area will help you define your strengths as well as how you can leverage those strengths. They'll also show your weaknesses and how you can minimize them for faster growth.

This exercise will also help you determine what percent of the market your competitors have—as well as why they have it and what you need to do to increase your share of that market. This allows you to project what percent of the market you can expect to achieve. Just think about how a buyer will respond if you have $10 million in revenue today, but have a growth plan and known market size to get you to $100 million. If the buyer thinks they can get your company there faster, you'll get a higher multiple buyer when you exit just by having a growth plan!

### Step 4: Get Ready to Grow/Build Your Go-to-Market Campaign

Now that you know *who* you're marketing to, the size and spend of that market, what that market's buying habits are, and how you're going to be successful based on your SWOT, you need to develop a go-to-market campaign to reach that market. This goes into Marketing 101 and how to present your products and services via print, social media, email, trade shows, sales on the street, etc. Remember to build and track your plan and adjust as needed. It is not one and done. It takes an average of ten touches for a prospect to get to know you.

---

It takes an average of ten touches for
a prospect to get to know you.

---

Start with your current clients. Look to expand your offering within other departments, and ask those clients for referrals. Take your new prospects and start with a wow offering to attract them. What is your best-selling product or service? Show your new prospects case studies from other clients to highlight a positive story about someone who bought your product or service. If you're concerned about confidentiality, don't list client names, simply state the industry and client title. Provide a "no worries" offer: if they're not happy, it's free. This will make you stand out. Commit to ten touches per prospect. Try test mailings with different offers and measure responses before launching a large mailing.

These four tips are a great start for developing a growth plan and will make your business more attractive to potential buyers. I'll go into greater detail about how to position your company for a sale in Chapter 5. Remember, growth planning should be a part of your exit strategy early on.

To learn more about how to grow a company by implementing one-to-one marketing programs, read *The One to One Field Book* by Don Peppers, Martha Rogers, and Bob Dorf.

# ⇒ SWOT CHART

## INTERNAL FACTOR: MANAGEMENT

### Strengths

→ Experienced senior leadership in place

→ Long-standing relationships with key accounts in similar industry

→ Existing operating platform with some accounts

### Weaknesses

→ Dependency on owner for sales leadership, management, driving client-centric experience

→ **Action:** hire seasoned sales professional to expand sales

## INTERNAL FACTOR: OFFERINGS

### Strengths

→ Profitable manufacturing

→ Have design tools in place that are easy to modify for B2B to C to market quickly

→ Have capacity with current equipment and specific tools to springboard the transition

### Weaknesses

→ Bandwidth in IT for web-based and mobile experience

→ **Action:** establish an outsource partner to expand bandwidth

## INTERNAL FACTOR: MARKETING

### Strengths

→ Relationship with strong brands that are currently the majority of sales

→ Company able to fund reasonable marketing initiatives

### Weaknesses

→ Little to zero brand awareness or formal marketing plan/budget in place

→ **Action:** need marketing experience for service team members

## INTERNAL FACTOR: PERSONNEL

### Strengths

→ Experienced, client-centric personnel on staff and readily transferable for new offerings

### Weaknesses

→ Lacking client services bandwidth with current workflow time requirements

→ **Action:** establish a bench of temp staff that can fill in work loads

## INTERNAL FACTOR: FINANCE

### Strengths

→ Company able to fund market expansion

→ Higher profit margins will help company quickly recover from the start-up investment

→ Economies of scale will allow for competitive pricing

### Weaknesses

→ Dependencies on one large client

→ Economic pressures depressing print industry

→ **Action:** fund a marketing campaign to attract new clients and mitigate risk of one

## INTERNAL FACTOR: MANUFACTURING

### Strengths

→ Equipment in place to run 24/7

→ Economies of scale improve for production process/pricing

→ Strong QC in place in shipping

### Weaknesses

→ Outsourcing caused QC problems

→ **Action:** look to add equipment to do it all inside

## INTERNAL FACTOR: IT–RD

### Strengths

→ Technology and staff experience is in place for this offering

### Weaknesses

→ IT bandwidth to implement new products/services

→ **Action:** seek outside source to build new offering

## EXTERNAL FACTOR: CLIENT

### Strengths

→ Looking for an extension of the marketing department for implementation and ideas

→ Intense competition for customers has created a need for nontraditional marketing distribution channels with all options available at one stop

### Weaknesses

→ Other providers offering similar solutions

→ Industry consolidation activities can erode existing client relationships

→ **Action:** build growth plan to attract new clients

## EXTERNAL FACTOR: COMPETITIVE

### Strengths

→ Proven product needs for these services and delivery model

→ Economies of scale support competitive pricing

→ Reputation as a high-level service provider will help convert business

### Weaknesses

→ Client service sales time and slower revenue ramp

→ **Action:** build a workflow to support a low-touch, scalable platform

## EXTERNAL FACTOR: TECHNOLOGICAL

### Strengths

→ Products are a ready-made solution without investing development dollars

→ The core products are resistant to changes

### Weaknesses

→ Offering needs to decrease human touch points, order entry, and production workflow

→ **Action:** build with client's ease of use

## EXTERNAL FACTOR: ECONOMIC

### Strengths

→ Current economic pressures are forcing corporate and end users to find cost-saving solutions to continue to provide a variety of competitive tools to the field

### Weaknesses

→ Companies may want to handle directly instead of outsource

→ **Action:** understand the markets and what drives them, keep a pulse on their trends, and look to diversify in adjacent markets

# NO REGRETS
## JOURNAL ENTRY

**LIST WHICH MARKET OR MARKETS YOU'RE CUR-
RENTLY IN.** Now, list the market or markets you should be in.

_____

_____

_____

_____

_____

**LIST YOUR AVAILABLE MARKET SIZE.** What percent of this
market do you have and what are your goals for capturing more of this
market?

_____

_____

_____

_____

_____

_____

_____

**COMPLETE A SWOT ANALYSIS.** What growth-related actions do you need to take to get to your goal?

_____

_____

_____

_____

_____

_____

**COMMIT TO A MARKETING CAMPAIGN.** What will it look like? How will you stick to it? How will you measure it?

_____

_____

_____

_____

_____

_____

_____

# CHAPTER 3

# CONSIDER EMOTIONS

*"Don't simply retire from something;*
*have something to retire to."*

— HARRY EMERSON FOSDICK

**ON JUNE 13, 1999, THE NIGHT BEFORE** the Alternatives sale, I didn't sleep. I sat at home worried about what would happen the next day. What would my employees do? What would Alternatives look like once the buyer took over? What would my customers think? In the early hours of the Alternatives sale, I was a complete wreck. The appeal of the large check I was about to receive had disappeared, and my emotions were anything but happy and positive. Nothing felt right. Not the decisions I'd made about the sale, or the sale itself.

The next morning, I signed Alternatives over to the buyer from the confines of a sterile, heartless building. I then left the high-rise to tell the eighty employees who were my friends about the sale. Because I hadn't developed an exit strategy, I didn't completely understand why I was selling Alternatives, whether I was selling at the right time, or what was going to happen to Alternatives, my employees, or myself.

Fast-forward sixteen years and many life lessons later. Once again, I was waiting to sell a company, but before this sale, I had an exit strategy in place. It was January 14, 2015, and instead of second-guessing myself alone at home the night before the sale, I sat at a local Minneapolis restaurant enjoying a world-famous almond crusted walleye while talking and laughing with the soon-to-be buyers of my company. I was selling a portion of the company I co-owned—Range Inc.—to publicly held Deluxe Corporation, which is one of the largest check printers in the United States and a provider of marketing materials to millions of small businesses. Range was a wholesale and local printing company that had a printing arm and a marketing and communications asset. Deluxe was about to buy the marketing and communications asset.

While we ate, the buyer's representatives asked detailed questions about my future plans. They also asked how I thought my employees might *feel* about the sale. As I sat at that table with my partner, they asked how we felt about the growth proposed for the company after the sale; whether we had concerns about the paperwork we would be signing the next day; how we felt about telling our employees about the sale; and how they could help us with that process. I couldn't believe how enjoyable the conversation or the process was. After sixteen years of buying and selling businesses, I finally realized a sale could be amicable, enjoyable, and fun.

Unlike the morning before the Alternatives sale, the night before the Range sale I felt great. I was 100 percent at peace with the decision I had made, happy that I had the right buyer, and really looking forward to announcing the sale.

---

## The emotional considerations of a sale address how the decisions you'll make about the sale will affect you, your employees, and the future of your company.

---

While selling the marketing portion of Range ended up *not* being my most lucrative sale, emotionally it was far and away the best sale I've ever made. Alternatives, on the other hand, was one of the more financially lucrative sales, but was emotionally the worst deal I've ever made.

Not only did I leave Merrill well before my contract expired, to this day, that sale continually reminds me how important it is to be prepared for a sale, know what to ask for during the sales process, and consider emotional elements before selling.

## WHAT ARE EMOTIONAL CONSIDERATIONS?

The emotional considerations of a sale address how the decisions you'll make about the sale will affect you, your employees, and the future of your company. While the financial outcome of a sale may seem like the most important component of it, if you don't consider the cause and effect of your choices during the sale, you risk leaving the sale filled with regrets.

I changed from having an almost unbearable tension and anxiety about selling Alternatives to a having a sense of absolute calm and accomplishment about selling Range because I was prepared for the Range sale. I was prepared for what would be asked during the selling process, had all the documents in order before Deluxe asked a single question, and knew how they envisioned growth for the company and the employees.

The way I felt before the Alternatives sale and the way I felt before the Range sale had nothing to do with my attachment to Alternatives or Range. Nor did it have to do with either buyer; both were great public companies. The difference had everything to do with *me* and the fact that I finally transitioned from being a *reactive* seller to a *proactive* one.

---

# RANGE VS. ALTERNATIVES

### Range

- Developed an exit strategy
- Defined ideal buyer
- Outlined the perfect sale

### Alternatives

- Did not develop an exit strategy
- Jumped at the first offer
- Didn't think about a worst-case/best-case sales scenario

---

## A CASE STUDY: RANGE VERSUS ALTERNATIVES

You don't have to wait sixteen years to move from being a reactive seller to being a proactive seller. Let's look at one of my best (Range) and one of my worst (Alternatives) sales emotionally and see how an exit strategy made the difference between the two.

When I acquired an interest in Range Printing in 2010, it was a forty-five-year-old Minnesota-based wholesale and local printing company that had been family run for years. Range had been riding a three-year national downturn in the printing industry driven by technological disruptions. The owners were second- and third-generation owners. The second generation was tired of riding the roller coaster that was common in that industry at the time and wanted to retire. The third generation held a minority position and had been working at Range since he was eight years old; he had no interest in leaving, but wasn't in a position to take over at that time.

Before I bought into Range, the owners had almost sold to another buyer, but they pulled out when they discovered the buyer's intention to manage the accounts from different locations, meaning nearly all Range employees would have lost their jobs. These owners had clearly thought through what they wanted from a sale before jumping at the first offer. They realized they absolutely did not want employees to lose their jobs. They also knew their son wanted to stay on and didn't want the manufacturing location to move.

When I bought Range, I lived in Dallas. My exit strategy from the start was to stay remotely involved, increase revenues, and get out within three to five years. For the first year following the sale, the third-generation owner and I ran Range with some input from a friend and investor. However, our sales growth remained flat, and when Range continued needing additional cash infusions, I decided to adjust my exit strategy and my *won't*, which was that I wouldn't move. I decided to leave Texas and move to Minnesota to become more active in the company.

## HOW REVISITING AN EXIT STRATEGY HELPS

After about three years, we doubled revenue, achieving a forty-eight-year sales high. Things were going well for the company, but I was headed down a path I didn't want to go down. I'd invested in Range for financial reasons and wasn't interested in running it long term, so I took a step back and revisited my exit plans.

My partners and I needed an exit strategy that would work for each of us, so we sat down and talked about what we really wanted. Why did I want to leave, and what did I want to do? What did my partners want? What did our solutions look like? Before selling Range, we looked before we leapt. We discussed our exit strategy and thought about what Range needed to look like before a sale and what it might look like after a sale.

After that initial conversation, it was clear that the third-generation owner loved running the manufacturing side of Range. He didn't want to leave the business. The other partner and I originally wanted to be investors; however, we ended up becoming too involved. Eventually, we had to review our exit strategy and what it would look like for *all* of us.

## HOW HAVING AN EXIT STRATEGY LEAVES NO REGRETS

As we walked through the exit strategy questions outlined in Chapter 1, we went through our why, what, when, and won't. Then we developed our Plan A and Plan B.

Our Plan A was to look into an employee stock ownership plan (ESOP). This would have prevented Range from being chopped up or dissolved while also giving our employees a future they would be able to control. This would have allowed me to exit financially, while giving my partner the ability to continue running Range manufacturing with his employees as partners. The problem with our Plan A was that the majority of our employees were older, and the manufacturing side of Range wasn't making much money. Because ESOPs operate on profit sharing and need higher earners to pay back the debt, an ESOP was an unlikely option.

Knowing that our Plan A was unlikely, we started developing our Plan B, beginning with what we didn't want. We knew based on market history that finding a competitor or another manufacturer as a buyer would likely mean some sort of consolidation. It would hinder my partner's ability to run the manufacturing side of Range, and would harm our employees, likely resulting in job loss. None of us wanted that. Knowing what we *didn't want* for the company, we again looked at what each of us wanted.

## FIND A SOLUTION THAT WORKS FOR ALL PARTNERS

Because I viewed Range as an investment, I had a price tag I wanted for the sale and planned exit. We were growing, and I didn't see any point in selling for a price we didn't think was reasonable. So for me, our price point was something we had to seriously consider.

Therefore, our Plan B was to find a strategic buyer to buy the marketing side. We wanted a cash purchase for the marketing side and wanted to give the manufacturing side a contract to manufacture the print work. The goal was to keep Range manufacturing intact. The third-generation owner would own that portion fully, and our manufacturing employees would remain in a role they enjoyed.

## HOW NOT HAVING AN EXIT STRATEGY CAN LEAD TO REGRETS

Whereas the Range sale had a Plan A and Plan B, I had only developed a Plan A for the Alternatives sale; it resembled the Plan A for the SCR sale, meaning it was based on the plan the seller offered rather than my own plan.

For a little background, I started Alternatives after the SCR sale went through specifically to help clients who had fallen through the cracks when Jostens took over SCR. As SCR struggled to fit into Jostens and some of my largest customers started downsizing, I had to find ways to cut costs for those customers. They no longer wanted to go to one printer for yearbooks and another for multi-colored printing. They said, "Listen, Paul. You know our brand requirements. You've got to do it all." They wanted a one-stop shop for all their printing needs. I designed Alternatives to do just that. By using Apple's desktop publishing, I was able to produce various materials for clients at a cost of about 20 percent less than competitors.

When I sold Alternatives, Plan A was that we would operate a standalone. At the time, the buyer was buying regional companies similar to Alternatives and letting each of those companies operate as they were. The benefit, of course, was that the buyer would offer financial power and give Alternatives a national footprint. The buyer's recent West Coast acquisition was doing well. The operator there assured me that the buyer had virtually left them alone to conduct business as usual.

Following my conversation with the West Coast acquisition, I failed to think about Alternatives's location in comparison to the buyer's. The buyer's corporate headquarters was in our backyard. It was literally right by us with a production plant and fulfillment facility that was just an hour away. The West Coast facility, which had been left alone up to that point, wasn't close to corporate and had logistics on their side. In hindsight, my Plan B should have considered these logistics. *My* Plan B should have considered the questions, "The buyer is right in your backyard. What happens if it decides to move production into its nearby facilities? How will that impact *my* employees, *my* role in the company, and *my* customers?"

## NEVER MAKE ASSUMPTIONS

With Alternatives, I assumed the buyer would do with us what it had done with the West Coast acquisition, but after the sale, the buyer realized it could save money if it consolidated Alternatives's fulfillment center into theirs. Alternatives had always done its own fulfillment, and we assumed we would be able to continue doing this after the sale. The buyer's decision to consolidate was something I should have considered before the sale and factored into the deal. If I'd asked the right questions *before* the sale and the buyer had said it wanted to buy Alternatives *specifically* to consolidate and leverage that cost savings, I would have brokered a different deal or used that information to negotiate my terms.

> ## NO REGRETS TIP
> Ask questions early, well before you close, especially regarding any plans to consolidate.

The consolidation dramatically affected our customers and the salespeople who worked for Alternatives. Many salespeople and customers left. These were really traumatic, emotionally challenging departures. I vividly remember one customer coming to me at one point and saying, "Paul, you promised this would be better for us, but it's far worse. Now what do we do?"

When people talk about that kicked-in-the-gut feeling following the sale of their business, they're talking about these situations. Even though sixteen years have passed since that client and I spoke, I still remember that conversation. I could have prevented that situation by having developed an exit strategy. Alternatives *was no longer mine* and, even though I was still working for the buyer, I no longer called the shots. Every decision regarding Alternatives's future and the future of my clients and employees rested with the buyer. For me, this was difficult to watch, but I couldn't blame the buyer. Alternatives was their company, and they had the right to make the decisions affecting it. Because I hadn't planned for the sale, I didn't understand the possibilities or ask the questions that could have avoided the heartache experienced by the clients, the employees, the buyer, and me.

## HOW TO AVOID JUMPING AT THE FIRST OFFER

When I sold Alternatives, I made another huge mistake: I jumped at the first offer. I liked that the buyer was a public company because it would give us the financial strength to grow internationally. I was also terrified that if I didn't jump at the buyer's offer, the buyer would disappear and no one else would make one. I also worried that my competitors would hear that I was selling and would use this information to take my clients. I thought I should sell quickly, which meant going with the first offer. Here's a lesson I've learned over and over again: More often than not, the first offer you get from a buyer is *not* going to be the best one for you, your employees, or your clients.

By the time I went into the Range sale, I had the benefit of sixteen years of hindsight. Because I knew what I did and did not want from the sale, saying no to the first few offers was easy. I wasn't disillusioned by the excitement of cash on the table or worried that if we didn't sell immediately, we never would. I knew that if we waited, something that was right for us would come along.

I passed on the first few offers for Range because the price didn't fit my exit strategy or one of my partner's end goals. Eventually, one of the companies I refused returned with a new bid. Soon after, we had a bidding war among a few companies so that fear I had at Alternatives—that passing on the first offer meant no sale—certainly wasn't true.

With the Alternatives sale, I was pretty certain the buyer we ended up selling to was our best fit and didn't want anyone else to know about it. I didn't want any more bids because I was afraid of market exposure. Putting hopes in one buyer and tuning out other possible buyers is a fairly common mistake many sellers make, especially if they expect that one company will make an offer close to the number they want. The seller doesn't want to rock the boat, so they stay quiet. This may seem logical, but it's actually a huge risk.

To this day, I don't know what other possibilities may have come my way had I waited for someone else to make an offer on Alternatives. I can say with some certainty that I wouldn't have had the emotional regrets I had by jumping at the first offer and selling too fast.

## HOW AN EXIT STRATEGY CAN LEAD TO A BETTER SALE

Interestingly, because we spent time planning our whys, whats, whens, and won'ts, we changed the direction of the Range sale.

Originally, Deluxe was going to buy the whole company; however, we worried that Deluxe might liquidate the manufacturing side, which would have put a lot of people out of work.

When I bought Range, the average tenure of its employees was twenty years, and I felt like an outsider. Even though I was a majority shareholder and my son and daughter-in-law worked there, I wasn't as emotionally attached to the business or the employees as my partner was. However, I did know what it was like to end a business feeling like I'd broken up a family, so when my partner voiced his concerns, I listened.

## HOW AN EXIT STRATEGY BRINGS ALL OPTIONS TO THE TABLE

As we talked through why we didn't want to sell all of Range to Deluxe, it came to light that the best option would be to sell a portion of Range—the marketing and communications assets—to Deluxe. As I mentioned before, Range was really two businesses—a marketing company and a manufacturing facility. Initially, Deluxe was interested in buying both pieces; however, when the buyer started wavering about including the manufacturing side in the sale, it worked out well for my partner and me. Our exit strategy made two things apparent. One, we didn't want a buyer dissolving the manufacturing side and moving the rest of the company; two, we wanted to monetize the growth so both of us could do what we wanted to do.

When we sold the marketing side of Range, the manufacturing side stayed intact. I stayed on in the manufacturing side as an investor until my partner was able to buy me out, and the result perfectly aligned with both of our goals. By returning to our exit strategy, we changed the structure of our sale to reflect what everyone wanted, thereby forgoing the regrets that would have occurred had the buyer bought both pieces of Range and dissolved the manufacturing side of it.

## HOW AN EXIT STRATEGY BENEFITS EMPLOYEES

The exit strategy we developed for Range also helped us do what was right for our employees. Before the sale, we spent time with the buyer's human resources department mapping employees so we could successfully transition each employee. The buyer's pay grades were different than ours. If one employee was at the top of a pay grade, the buyer started them at the lower end of a higher pay grade so they had more room for growth. As a result, after the sale, several of our employees actually got a pay increase. This step was instrumental in ensuring our employees were taken care of from the start. They appreciated it, and this decision made the transition much easier.

With the Alternatives sale, I didn't know to have detailed conversations with the buyer's human resources department about what employee compensation might look like or what would happen to each employee. When it became clear that the buyer was going to absorb our accounting team, I negotiated a payment for some of Alternatives's key accounting roles. Unfortunately, I didn't have the experience or the foresight to ask about what would happen to other roles, such as our sales staff, whose noncompetes were affected by the sale.

About thirty days after I sold Alternatives, the buyer asked the sales team to sign new noncompetes. Our noncompetes were not written like the buyer's, and it made sense to them for the agreements to match. However, I should have asked whether sales staff needed to resign before the sale and then built a signing bonus or given them a percentage of my earnout as an incentive for them to sign the new agreement. Because they had to re-sign noncompetes, meaning theirs were no longer in effect, several of our salespeople left to compete with us, which was the beginning of the end in terms of the employees transitioning out of Alternatives. I didn't know which questions to ask the buyer. If I'd known what to ask, I could have put my employees in a much better position post-sale.

> ## NO REGRETS TIP
> Protect your employees presale. If I'd known
> what to ask, I could have put my employees in
> a much better position post-sale.

With the Range sale, I really examined employee benefits. I made sure Deluxe had comparable benefits. I also ensured our employees could continue going to the same doctors. Before the Alternatives sale, I made sure my employees would have benefits, but wasn't intimately involved in what they would look like, which didn't work out the best for my employees. Again, another lesson learned.

## HOW AN EXIT STRATEGY ENDS IN CELEBRATION

Unlike the Alternatives sale, the Range sale ended in celebration. We set aside a day for the signing, which was over in about thirty minutes because of all the pre-planning we did. We waited until the next day to tell the employees and introduce them to the new buyer, which I'll talk about in greater detail later.

Because I had asked numerous questions about our employees and our culture to make sure both were taken care of before the sale was final, I knew our employees would fit in well with the buyer's culture. I knew they would be taken care of and wouldn't experience the culture shock and disappointment that comes with a quick and dramatic change in company culture. I also knew many Range employees would either have higher salaries than before or go from part- to full-time work. The transition went so smoothly that several employees thanked me for keeping the culture and their benefits after we closed.

As a whole, the aftermath of the Range sale was celebratory. The aftermath of the Alternatives sale was filled with remorse. In fact, the Alternatives sale announcement was somewhat ominous and depressing. Someone from the buyer's corporate office came to Alternatives and spoke corporate-speak about the sale that none of the employees understood. Not long after, employees started complaining about the sterile atmosphere, and I started looking to leave. I was supposed to stay on for five years, but after a year, I left. I forfeited my rights to the balance of my five-year earnout and guaranteed employment contract.

## AVOID REGRETS: ASK THE RIGHT QUESTIONS

The disappointment my employees and I experienced after the Alternatives sale wasn't the buyer's fault. It was mine. I was too naïve to develop an exit strategy and ask certain questions of the buyer—questions about things like company culture and the outcome for my sales team.

Of all the moving parts that must fall into place to sell a business, preparedness will save you from making *huge* mistakes and shouldering a mountain of regrets. The only way to do this is to develop your why, what, when, and won't.

Throughout the remainder of *No Regrets*, we'll return to Alternatives and Range because there's no better teacher than past experience. While my experience with the Alternatives sale taught me how *not* to sell a business, my experience with the Range sale taught me how to sell a business without regrets.

## NO REGRETS
## JOURNAL ENTRY

**WHAT DOES YOUR IDEAL SALE LOOK LIKE?** Write what your best sale would look like. What would the buyer look like? How will you feel? How will your employees feel? Who are the key employees you want to protect post-sale? What will the culture be? What will you net from the sale? What do you see yourself doing after the sale?

_____

_____

_____

_____

_____

_____

**WHAT DOES YOUR WORST SALE LOOK LIKE?** What would the buyer look like? How will you and your employees feel following that sale? What would you net from that sale? What can you do now to prevent this scenario? How will you adjust your exit strategy to prevent this from happening?

_____

_____

_____

_____

_____

_____

**WHAT DOES A GOOD DAY VERSUS A BAD DAY AT YOUR COMPANY LOOK LIKE?** What makes a day good or bad? Do they stay the same or change? What can you do so you don't leave during a bad day or bad year filled with regrets?

_____

_____

_____

_____

_____

_____

_____

_____

_____

_____

_____

_____

_____

_____

_____

_____

# SECTION 2

# FIND A BUYER

# CHAPTER 4

➡

# UNDERSTAND
# PRESALE PLANNING

*"Setting a goal is not the main thing. It is deciding how you will go about achieving it and staying with that plan."*

— Tom Landry

**WHEN I SOLD RANGE,** the first thing I did after developing an exit strategy was rally my advisory team, or as I like to call them, my A-Team. Rallying your A-Team is sort of like picking players for a championship football team. Choose your top players wisely because they're the ones who will help you execute your game plan—in this case, your exit strategy—so you win.

---

Choose your top players wisely because
they're the ones who will help you
execute your game plan—in this case,
your exit strategy—so you win.

---

Your A-Team is an objective trio of professionals who have unique skills to help get you through the sale. Specifically, your team will include a business advisor (also known as business broker or investment banker), an attorney, and an accountant. Your A-Team is not only best suited to handle the details of the sale, but when it comes to negotiations, they will also be the only objective party acting on your behalf. It is difficult for a seller to remove emotions from the selling process, which can dramatically and negatively impact the outcome of a sale. An advisor, however, can. This is why it's critical to build your A-Team the minute you decide you want to sell.

I bet you can guess what my A-Team looked like going into the Alternatives sale. It was non-existent. While I worked with an investment banker and lawyer on the sale, we didn't work as a team. Through no fault of their own, I hired both without really thinking about their areas of expertise or how they aligned with what I hoped to get from the sale, nor did they. Your A-Team is critical to your presale planning process, so do your research and find a team that will work best for you.

## NO REGRETS TIP

Your A-Team is critical to your presale planning process so do your research and find a team that will work best for you.

### WHAT IS PRESALE PLANNING?

Once you've decided it is time to sell your business and have developed the why, what, when, and won't of your exit strategy, you'll start the presale planning process. Presale work is a three-step process that includes building your A-Team, confirming your company valuation against your advisor's valuations and accessing the gaps and ways to mitigate those gaps, and gathering all financial documents needed so you can quickly present them to a qualified buyer. If you do this, when a buyer calls, you can hand them the information they need without distracting your team from running your business.

## THREE THINGS TO DO DURING PRESALE PLANNING

→ Build your A-Team

→ Confirm your company valuation against your advisor's valuations and access the gaps and ways to mitigate those gaps

→ Gather all financial documents needed so you can quickly present them to a qualified buyer

Returning to the analogy that selling a business is like selling a house, think of your exit strategy as the equivalent of making a decision to sell. Once you decide it's *time* to sell, you have to get the house *ready* to sell. You have to prepare to put that "for sale" sign in the yard. You've got to focus on the curb appeal and fix up those little things you meant to get around to that will add more value to the house so potential buyers immediately find it attractive. You also need to gather information about the house—when the water heater was last replaced, the age of the roof, and on and on—so the majority of a buyer's questions are answered when they take their first look. No one wants to look at a house with a crumbling roof and leaking water heater. They want to look at the picture of perfection so they can visualize themselves spending the rest of their lives in that home. The same principle applies to selling your business. Your buyer needs to be able to picture themselves working within it for years to come.

To put that for sale sign in your yard, you need to bring on the right partners, value your business, and get your documents in order. Failing to do any of these three things may result in a viable buyer walking away from your business. It may also result in a sale that isn't financially or emotionally beneficial to you, your employees, or your family.

### STEP 1: CHOOSE YOUR A-TEAM

If you had to go to court, would you hire a lawyer or defend yourself? What about filing your taxes? If you owned a multimillion-dollar company, would you do the filing yourself or would you hire a professional? Chances are, you'd hire a professional.

Because most sellers don't understand the process of selling a business—that it's much more involved then slapping a for sale ad on the Internet—they don't know enough to put the sale together themselves. Many books about selling businesses get into nitty-gritty details about selling. These details are better managed by a team of professionals. It's your job to hire those professionals. It's your job to carefully pick that A-Team of advisor, attorney, and accountant.

### Sign Confidentiality Agreements

One of the first things you should do before talking to other parties about selling is make sure that both parties sign confidentiality or nondisclosure agreements. These agreements ensure that neither party shares information about the sale as you move through the sales process.

### Choose an Advisor

Your advisor is the leader, or the quarterback, of your A-Team and is, therefore, the most important hire. This advisor may be a business broker, an investment banker, or a mergers and acquisitions (M&A) firm. Each essentially does the same thing; however, some have larger teams. The size of the team typically coincides with the size of the company, so the larger the company, the larger the team.

Your advisor will market your business by helping develop your marketing plan, designing your marketing materials, and creating marketing campaigns that will be useful when you go to market. He or she will also vet each interested buyer's ability to close a sale, keep the sale confidential, and negotiate the terms objectively, without the emotions you as a seller might have getting in the way. Your advisor is in the foxhole with you. They are there to watch your back and make sure you come out with the best deal possible financially and emotionally.

The type of advisor you hire will depend on the type of your business, the size of your business, and the outcome you want from the sale. How you choose your advisor will largely depend on your chemistry with the advisor, the size of the sale, the type of service offered, the buyer, and the level of expertise needed for the sale.

### Have the Right Chemistry

Having chemistry with your advisor is absolutely critical. You'll spend countless hours with this person so, at the very least, you must like the advisor and respect his or her knowledge base. You also need to trust that when you're in the heat of battle—when negotiations are flying back and forth—that the advisor will understand exactly what you want and fight for your end goals.

### Consider the Size of the Sale

While advisors essentially do the same thing, some are better equipped to handle main street deals—that is, deals that range from $100,000 to $5 million. Others are better equipped to handle mid-market deals ranging from $5 million to $50 million or public and larger deals of $50 million or more.

Your specific needs related to the sale will also impact who you hire as an advisor. While one advisor may specialize in raising capital, another might be better suited for an ESOP or growth strategies through acquisitions.

## NO REGRETS TIP
Find the right advisor. It is important that your advisor understands you and your needs above anything else.

### Consider the Type of Buyer

The type of buyer—private, public, synergistic, financial—that you desire will also affect which type of advisor you hire, as will the level of expertise you need from this advisor. One advisor might excel at marketing and working with public companies, while another might focus on procuring sales within a certain industry.

It's more important that you trust that he or she understands what you need, will go to battle for you when the negotiations start, and always has your best interest at heart.

### A Sale without an A-Team

When I sold Alternatives, I had no experience, no guidance, no idea what the selling process was like, and no idea what I wanted from the sale. I ended up going with an investment banker as an advisor. He had sold another business in my industry so I thought he'd be the right fit for the Alternatives sale, too. I assumed that experience selling within a certain industry was all that mattered. That was a mistake. It was like listing a house with a realtor who knows the area versus listing with one who really knows the real-estate industry, the market, and how to market a specific type of home within that market.

I knew my business and my market, but didn't know anything about marketing it for sale so I hired an advisor because I thought any one would yield the same results. I gave my advisor my listing, he stuck the sign in the yard—which in my case meant making a few calls—and I then had an offer to look at. When you're selling a business, this tactic can be dangerous. It can lead to results that have nothing to do with your exit strategy, which, of course, ends in regrets.

> Whatever your particular needs are, no matter what size or type of business you're selling, hiring the right advisor for your sale is a critical component of presale planning.

*I* should have found an advisor better suited for my situation. *I* should have gone with someone who would have asked if I had an exit strategy—I didn't. The right advisor would have said, "We can't start this process without an exit strategy." The right advisor would have asked if I wanted to stay on after the sale, what I'd want my role to be, whether I'd considered that the buyer might consolidate, and what I wanted for my employees. He or she would have asked, "How do each of these elements impact sales price?" Whatever your particular needs are, no matter what size or type of business you're selling, hiring the right advisor for your sale is a critical component of presale planning. Their expertise is their value. It's what will guide you through the sale. They should look at your exit strategy and make sure that your sales outcome aligns with that strategy.

### An A-Team Kind of Sale

Unlike the Alternatives sale, for the Range sale I found an investment banker that was perfect for what we wanted, and we were able to tell him what we did and did not want from the sale. The investment banker advised me well, but I also was prepared before we hired him. I knew what questions to ask of him.

Deciding what you want from the sale will impact your selling price. Good advisors understand this, and they work hard to ensure you don't simply get the best deal in terms of dollars and cents, but that you get the best outcome for you—one that follows your exit strategy and leaves no regrets.

### You Get What You Pay For

Far too many sellers forgo an advisor because they think they'll save money if they do the deal themselves. Let's return to that real estate example. People hire realtors because they know how to market, know how to price houses, and can often find buyers the homeowner wouldn't find if they just stuck a for sale sign in the yard. They provide value. The same is true of an advisor. Sure, you will pay your advisor a percentage of the sale or a success fee, but a good one is worth his or her weight in gold. They get you more than you expected, which will offset their fee so you net more. Not only can advisors get a better financial outcome for your sale, they can make sure your sale aligns with your exit strategy so you leave with no regrets. This is particularly important if you decide to stay on because negotiations can get heated and having your advisor's clear head during them is valuable.

Without an advisor, you'll quickly get buried in requests about the sale that will pull your attention away from your business, potentially harming your value. An advisor will guide you through the sales process so it does not consume your time. He or she will also step in when your emotions get in the way of a negotiation. For example, the advisor might tell you when to stop arguing a point and then show you how it doesn't benefit you or your exit strategy.

As the quarterback of your sale, your advisor will not only direct a sale that aligns with your exit strategy goals, but he or she will also advise when—and if—you need to hire additional team members. When this occurs, your advisor may recommend a few attorneys and accountants known to have good reputations in your area and who *specialize* in the type of advice you need.

---

Think about valuation in terms of how both you *and* the buyer will value your company.

---

### Hire Your Other Aces

Your **accountant**, who will likely be a tax specialist, will help with the valuation of your business, audit your numbers, and make sure your generally accepted accounting principles (GAAP) are in order. A tax specialist is critical for tax planning because he or she will clarify what you will actually net from the sale. The tax specialist understands an asset sale versus a stock sale, your investment basis, what you have in the business, and capital gains versus personal income and how that will impact your tax burden. He or she knows what you can expense and what you can't.

Not only can your advisor help you find a tax specialist, but he or she can also help you find an **attorney**. There are many types of law, but when it comes to selling, you want representation from a mergers and acquisitions specialist. These specialists understand the ins and outs of selling a business and can help the advisor negotiate with the buyer's attorney. The attorney drafts, reviews, edits, and revises agreements, including LOIs, purchase agreements, representations, and warrants.

## STEP 2: VALUATION: WHAT'S YOUR COMPANY WORTH?

In Chapter 1, we discussed the importance of having a baseline valuation and calculating that valuation from year to year. When you start preplanning for the sale of your company, you have to think about valuation in terms of how both you *and* the buyer will value your company. You will view your company very differently than potential buyers, and each of you will have different motivations for choosing your respective valuation methods.

Numerous books detail every way to value a company, but in the end, you will choose one way to value your company and the buyer will choose another. Valuating a company using different valuation methods can be like trying to solve a written math problem with only half the information.

The difference in valuation numbers between buyer and seller occurs for two reasons. One, numerous variables affect a valuation. Two, there are multiple ways, or valuation methods, to value a company. The buyer and seller each choose a way to value the company because it helps both parties consider what they would pay/accept for payment and shows where gaps exist in their value assessments. Closing these gaps is what negotiation is all about.

The first thing you and your advisor should look at during valuation are the variables that can affect valuation. Below is a list of common variables that can affect valuation.

### Variables:

→ **History**: How many years have you been in business? Are revenues growing or flat?

→ **Industry:** Is the market declining or growing?

→ **Revenue:** Is revenue contractual or transactional? Can you predict revenue?

→ **Pricing:** Is pricing commodity priced or do you have value added? Is it price sensitive or can it set market price?

→ **Location:** Can you grow where you are currently located? Are you landlocked? Is there a pool of employees available if you expand?

→ **Technology:** Is it scalable? Is it flexible so you can add services? Is it easy to tie in new financing systems, or would the buyer have to invest and revise your platform to fit his?

→ **Planning:** Do you have a strategic growth plan? What do you need to add to grow? Will that take a big or little investment?

→ **Operations:** What is the condition of your building? Are any renovations planned? What does your equipment list look like?

→ **Sales and Marketing:** Are the materials up to date? Can the sales team learn to sell additional products or services?

Don't be surprised if a buyer's numbers are different than yours. Remember, in addition to the numerous variables used to value a company, the buyer may have valued it completely differently. Maybe the buyer is used to buying companies and therefore uses a defined valuation model for every sale. The buyer may also feel the valuation method is easy for upper management and boards to understand. It's not uncommon for a buyer to subtract some of the variables above from his or her valuation of your company. Maybe the valuation model the buyer typically uses doesn't include elements that you've listed in your valuation. This has the potential to dramatically affect the buyer's valuation of your company.

When I sold Range, Deluxe used a very simple valuation method. It was a multiple of our average annual gross margin. Remember, we divided Range and sold a portion of it to Deluxe so the assets and liabilities associated with the manufacturing end—equipment, inventory, etc.—didn't go with Range. This made the valuation model fairly easy for both parties to use.

Of course, while each valuation has advantages and disadvantages for each party, every sale and valuation presents its own challenge. Although Range had few assets and liabilities, customers were an extremely important variable. To make our sales price work, the entire purchase price needed to be amortized over eight years. In order to do that, we had to show Deluxe we were not too leveraged by one or two key clients and that our overall client tenure averaged eight or more years. If we hadn't been able to prove this, it's likely the sale would have fallen through, as Deluxe probably would have had to amortize over fewer years and the ROI wouldn't have made the sale worthwhile to them.

### Consider the Top Three Valuation Methods

While the Range sale used a valuation based on a percentage of our average annual gross margin, this valuation method may not work for your sale. Let's take a look at three of the most common valuation methods used by buyers. These include EBITDA, which is the most common, gross margin, and revenue. Each has many factors that can impact the value as well as the multiplier that is added. Other valuation methods that are not as common or are more specific to certain types of companies include flow or discounted cash flow for service companies or asset sales for companies such as manufacturers.

### Model One: EBITDA

As we discussed in Chapter 1, EBITDA is a great way to determine baseline valuations.

This model works well for a variety of companies because a number of variables can be used.

#### How It Works

1. Take your average net income[1]

2. Add back interest expenses paid

3. Add back tax expenses paid

4. Add back depreciation expenses

5. Add back amortization expenses[2]

Actual net income plus these add backs equal your EBITDA. This will provide a baseline valuation. Keep in mind this option uses multiples that can typically range from three to eight times based on a company's history, tenure, and other factors. It is important that you use the same multiple—I recommend using three—year to year for your valuation. Possible add backs—such as additional owner's compensation above what you would pay someone to do your job, and extra perks such as cars, membership fees, fixed assets, or liabilities—can affect this valuation.

EBITDA models can have all kinds of additions or subtractions and can really swing valuations between a seller and a buyer. Typically, this model leads to more negotiations. For example, my Alternatives advisor valued the sale using a variation of EBITDA models. Using these models, he included add backs for additional owner's compensation on top of EBITDA and applied a multiple. The buyer used the EBITDA model differently than my advisor did and arrived at an EBITDA number that was similar with a slight adjustment to our

1   Use a minimum of three-year average. Your advisor may use three or five years with two years looking forward or back one, or a variety of ways to present your company in the best way based on the buyer. Your advisor will factor in whether you're growing and whether you were growing in the past. If you were not, the focus will be on the future. If you grew a lot in the past and are currently flat, your advisor may focus on the past.

2   Long-term clients show stability and give buyers a way to amortize the purchase over a longer period of time. This helps a buyer build post-acquisition models or a way to forecast future performance after acquisition costs, which makes the purchase look better for the buyer. This may yield a higher selling price for sellers who have long-term clients.

Find a Buyer

stated add backs. The buyer then added the difference of fixed assets from long-term debt and applied a smaller multiple.

Even though we used similar valuation models, there was a fairly large gap between the buyer's valuation and my advisor's valuation. We will take a closer look at how to close these types of gaps in Chapter 5. With the Alternatives sale, we ended up resolving this gap during negotiations. We agreed to an earnout as the best solution although, in hindsight, I didn't really know how to structure an earnout or what I would be able to control. A better option for that sale should have included reaching a different solution or looking to another buyer.

### Model Two: Multiple of Gross Margin

The gross margin model works well for nonmanufacturing-based service companies with minimum assets or debt.

*How It Works*

1. Total your three- or five-year annual gross margin[3]

2. Divide that total by the years used above (three or five)

3. Take the above number and apply a multiple[4]

4. Look at the baseline valuation, which you can build from

As we saw with the Range example, this valuation is fairly simple, but also may include numerous variables that will affect value.

### Model Three: Revenue

The revenue model works well for software as a service (SaaS) companies and high-growth companies.

*How It Works*

1. Calculate your average annual revenue over a three- to five-year period

2. Apply a multiplier of one to two, with one being short-term growth and two being used if you've had longer-term growth

3. Arrive at your baseline revenue valuation

---

3   Varies based on history, growth, and forecast.

4   Multiples are based on company history, client's tenure, contracts, etc.

Remember, there are almost as many ways to value your business as there are businesses. What works for your friend or a previous sale may be totally wrong for today's sale.

---

> Remember, there are almost as many ways to value your business as there are businesses.

---

## One Business, Three Valuation Outcomes

Let's take a look at how each of our three valuation models would change the value of a single business. For each example, let's assume our company is six years old and only over the last three years has seen both revenue and margin grow. The average revenue is $10 million, average gross margin is 40 percent, and average net income is 10 percent. Knowing that, let's look at how each of the three valuation models would work.

### Model One: EBITDA

Average of three years of revenue = $10 million
Net income (10 percent) = $1 million
Interest = $50,000
Tax = $200,000
Depreciation = $50,000
Amortization = $50,000
Owner's additional compensation = $100,000
Total of $1,450,000 after EBITDA add backs
Multiple of five x $1,450,000
**Value = $7.250 million**

### Model Two: Multiple of Gross Margin

Average three years of revenue = $10 million
Gross margin = $4 million (40 percent)
Apply a multiple of 1.5 to $4,000,000 (1.5 x $4,000,000)
**Value = $6 million**

## Model Three: Revenue

Average of three years' revenue = $10,000,000
Multiple of one (because of new growth and limited profitability)
**Value = $10 million**

As you can see, by using three methods without considering the many variables that go into the sale of a business, we have three valuations ranging from $6 million to $10 million.

## Use Your Valuation as a Baseline

When buyers value your company, they look at it from a very sterile point of view. Many sellers will have their accountant value their company, which is helpful for buy/sell agreements or insurance. However, the resulting valuation doesn't always reflect what a buyer will pay and could give the seller a false sense of what the company is worth. As a result, the seller may not fully understand what his or her company is *actually* worth to a particular buyer. When you get to package to market, I will show you how to value beyond just the black-and-white valuations. Your A-Team will review all options; consider your exit goals, buyer, market, and industry; and then present your company in the best possible light.

If the seller doesn't understand the valuation and a buyer approaches the seller, the seller may sell for too little. Or, the buyer may stop the process because he or she believes there's too big of a gap between the asking price and the current value of the company.

Business advisors can help provide a more accurate valuation based on the buyer, valuation variables, and the market's ability to present your company. They will consider each to help you devise a strategy for adding more value to potential buyers.

Advisors should have market knowledge, which can help you reach a more realistic valuation number. Even if you're not ready to sell *today*, an advisor can get you thinking about who might be interested in buying one, two, or three years down the road. The advisor also might know of a company that's for sale that could be a potential acquisition, which would thereby allow you to grow faster to achieve your goal of selling in the future.

## Always Return to Your Exit Strategy

Each of these valuations should only be used as a *baseline* for what your business is worth. They are a value gauge. How you go to market with your business should be based on your exit strategy goals, who you feel is your dream buyer, how you market, and how your final value is achieved.

For example, selling at a lower price and negotiating terms for key employees to stay on might be more valuable to a seller than a higher-priced deal that doesn't include those guarantees. In another example, say your company is valued at $10 million with an additional $2 million guaranteed for you to stay on for five years following the sale, the technical value would be $12 million. However, if you know you don't want to stay on—if your exit strategy has you moving on after the sale—you may be better off agreeing to a lower number and walking away.

During the valuation process, if *you* don't return to your exit strategy, which should clearly state what you will and will not accept in a deal, you risk walking out of a deal filled with emotional regrets. It may not be worth getting an extra $500,000 or $1 million if that gain goes against your exit strategy and the deal leaves you with emotional regrets.

Despite the various ways to value a company, the outcome you hope to get from the sale shouldn't be determined by valuation alone. It will also be determined by what you feel is a fair price, how you feel that outcome fits with your exit strategy, and what the buyer is willing to pay.

No matter which valuation method you choose, when you're comparing valuations from year to year, you have to compare apples to apples. You can't use gross margin in January and, after acquiring a new company in March, value your company based on a percentage of EBITDA. You will not have an accurate sense of how the value has changed. Failing to compare valuations based on the same model can result in a different valuation, which can affect your baseline valuation.

## STEP 3: GET YOUR DOCUMENTS IN ORDER

Your final presale planning step is to get your documents in order. Don't wait to do this until a buyer requests the documents. Oftentimes, sellers' documents are not in order, are inaccurate, or can't easily be found when the buyer asks for them. You have to quickly present professional, accurate documents. If it takes too long to gather your documents, you could lose a potential buyer. If the documents are not accurate, you lose creditability. The buyer needs to know that all those little fixes—the new paint on the exterior of the house, the landscaping—are finished. You need to shine before putting that for sale sign in the yard.

Everything the buyer sees—from your website to your marketing materials to the exterior of your building—will tell the story of your business. That story must align with the one you want to tell your buyer. You need to be organized, clean, and appealing. You need to show the buyer how well run your company is. This is done, in large part, through the documents you provide to the potential buyer. Your business plans must be updated with detailed growth plans. Debt agreements should include valuations on listed assets. Your company's financials must comply with GAAP, and your company meeting minutes should be up to date before you start marketing your company to potential buyers.

## Clean Up Balance Sheets

Critical pieces of documentation to clear up before going to potential buyers are your profit/loss statements and balance sheets. You must clear any odd one-off entries that don't tie into your business. For example, during the early days of Alternatives, I would at times loan key employees money. My accountant would place the loans on my balance sheet as a receivable asset. I had to clear those before selling Alternatives. During those early years, I also had too many line items on my profit/loss statements because it gave me more details into productivity. Most buyers that are not close to your business do not care about these details, so these numbers confuse things and should be rolled up for the buyers.

## Break Down Departments

Whether you decide to gather your documents electronically or by hand, make sure to break your documents down into departments—HR, legal, finance, operations, marketing, sales, client services, sourcing, real-estate facilities, technology, and distribution—and gather the data to support each statement within each department. This makes it much easier for the buyer to access the exact information he or she is looking for.

## Get Organized

In addition to selling businesses, I've bought numerous businesses. Nothing turns a buyer off more quickly than disorganized or missing documents. Many sellers use bookkeeping software such as QuickBooks to organize their documents. They think the fact that files exist within QuickBooks is enough for the seller. What they don't think about are the entries within QuickBooks that won't make any sense to the buyer. When I ask, "What's that?" you can't say, "Oh, that was a loan we gave to Uncle Frank three years ago." Your documents must be straightforward.

---

## Nothing turns a buyer off more quickly than disorganized or missing documents.

---

Software programs such as Smart Sheets can help organize these documents. Smart Sheets keeps documents in a confidential digital format that is easy to upload, edit, share, and track views and updates.

At a minimum, regardless of your business size or industry, most buyers will look for the following reports as broken down by topic:

### Company Overview

→ Years in business

→ How you make money

→ Type of business (i.e., manufacturing, service, wholesale, retail)

### Marketing

→ How you go to market

→ How you solve clients' needs

→ Brand standards and list of documents or items that have your brand on them

### Finance

→ Monthly profit/loss (P/L) statements for the last twelve months, year to date, and previous two years presented in an organized way that a buyer can understand

- Detailed revenue breakouts including GM, operating income (OI), and EBITDA
- Growth projections for three years
- A clean balance sheet
- Accounts receivable/accounts payable (AR/AP) for the last 120 days (make sure to write off any bad debt you may be carrying)

### Customers

- Top twenty customers and an overview of service, tenure, industry, and percentage of your revenue
- You can list Client A, Client B, Client C, etc., rather than listing the actual name of the client. Also note whether you have contracts with each client. This information can be very valuable when looking at amortizing the purchase.

### Technology

- Provide a list of the software you're using, an overview of systems you're using, workflow, processes, and a list of licenses
- Detailed process procedures to provide additional value

### HR Organization Chart

- Organizational charts for the entire company
- Job descriptions
- Departmental responsibilities overview that includes what each group does
- Employee manuals
- Review dates with history of increases

It's critical that as you build your document library, you also write out processes for each of your departments. What does Bob in accounts payable do and how does he do it? The point here is that even if you think you know your processes, a buyer will not. They will not know what to do if Bob leaves or goes on vacation. Remember, in many cases, buyers will bring your business into theirs. Detailed processes make this much easier to do. If your processes are not in place, a buyer may feel it's too difficult to integrate the two companies and will walk away from the deal or discount the price based on the additional expense of bringing the two companies together.

By going through these three preplanning steps—bringing on the right partners, confirming your valuations, and getting your documents in order—you help get a sale that follows your exit strategy and isn't financially or emotionally detrimental to you, your employees, or your family.

Find a Buyer

# NO REGRETS
# JOURNAL ENTRY

**CHOOSE YOUR A-TEAM.** Who do you have already? Who do you need to meet?

_____

_____

_____

_____

_____

_____

**CHOOSE A BASELINE VALUATION METHOD.** Either choose one from _No Regrets_ or use one you have been using already, but make sure you use the same one year over year. Journal the results and annually compare them to your exit strategy and "what" goal.

_____

_____

_____

_____

_____

_____

**EXAMINE YOUR DOCUMENTS.** Which ones don't you have? Which ones need to be clarified or produced? Develop a process to keep your files in order so they are ready to present to a buyer.

Find a Buyer

# CHAPTER 5

➡

# PREPARE TO
# PACKAGE TO MARKET

*"In the end, a vision without the ability to execute it is probably a hallucination."*

— STEVE CASE

**WHEN WE SOLD SCR,** the Heidelberg press was considered the Mercedes of printing presses. We thought it was our differentiator. However, after we sold SCR, we realized that most of our competitors could claim that they had the same press *and* high-quality service. Looking at those two measurements, we were all pretty much the same.

Most sellers base their value by presenting what they *believe* is their edge. They base their value based on the quality and price of their product or service or on what they can do for the customer to help the buyer find, grow, or retain customers. This is like selling a house based on the fact that it has a roof and four walls. If every other house has a roof and four walls, yours doesn't stand out. Nothing about your house differentiates you from other sellers.

If you try to sell your house based on the fact that *in addition to* four walls and a roof, it has a pool, but your buyer doesn't swim, you're still not providing a differentiator for your buyer. In this instance, a pool could actually be a deterrent for the buyer, who may not want to incur the expense to upkeep something he or she won't use.

Whether selling a house or a business, to sell to the right buyer, you need to really understand your edge in the marketplace and know that not every buyer needs or wants the same thing.

---

> To sell to the right buyer, you need to really understand your edge in the marketplace and know that not every buyer needs or wants the same thing.

---

In hindsight, we shouldn't have pitched SCR to Jostens based on the two differentiators that weren't actually differentiators. Instead, we should have packaged SCR in a variety of ways that would have mirrored the needs of potential buyers. We should have looked at SCR and said, "What is the best way to package SCR so we mirror the needs of the buyer—in this case, Jostens?"

## WHAT IS PACKAGE TO MARKET?

Package to market starts the process of building a marketing plan to help you find the right buyer for your business. This process tests your creative side in terms of who might be a buyer and how you can best show the additional value your company can bring them.

Package to market is the process that brings the why, what, when, and won't of your exit strategy as well as your presale planning valuation together to develop your marketing plan. This process defines what you need to accomplish before the sale to get what you want from it. So, if the baseline valuations we discussed in Chapter 4 are not congruent between buyer and seller, you will need to fill the gap by:

- → Revisiting when you want to sell
- → Determining whether you need to organically grow before you go to market, or
- → Deciding whether you should acquire another company to add more value to the buyer

This step of the sales process must align with why you built the company and what you feel the buyers may want.

## DEFINE YOUR UNIQUE VALUE

Think about the last time you edited your resume. You mirrored it to match the job posting, right? You highlighted your education, work experience, and accomplishments based on the job description. For another job description, you'd take the same education and experience and present it in a different way. If you think like this when you're ready to package to market, you will attract more buyers based on their individual interests. This requires getting creative, thinking outside the box, and looking at specific markets and how you can match the buyer's interest.

When I'm getting ready to package to market, I think of the spoon test that my dad taught me when I was in third grade and went to a dad/son workday. My dad's background was in engineering and he was in a unique position to lead the marketing efforts for Northfield, Minnesota-based aerospace company, GT Sheldahl. During our lunch break, dad explained marketing in the simplest terms possible. He said, "Son, see this spoon? If I invented it and only thought about it as something to pick up food with, people might say, 'I don't need it, I have a fork.' My job would be to figure out who would specifically need a spoon. Who would that be? Someone eating soup, right? People who eat soup would want a spoon so I'd want to sell my spoon to restaurants that sell soup. They would understand the value of that spoon over a fork. They would pay more for that spoon so their customers wouldn't spill soup all over the place. That, my son, is marketing!"

Your package to market is your spoon test. It helps you determine who might want your company. Return to it when you start building your list of prospective buyers because if you don't know what type of buyer you'd like or why they might want your company, you might end up building a company that nobody wants, selling a company you do want to the wrong buyer for less value than its worth, or completing a sale that doesn't align with your exit strategy.

## THINK LIKE A MARKETER

Thinking like a marketer means looking at what your company currently can do and seeing how you can apply that to another market. It's figuring out which other companies might need your spoon.

When I first started working with SCR in 1983, I struggled to get sales until I had an epiphany that involved identifying specific markets that needed similar services. SCR provided high-quality designs and printing through ad agencies, but hadn't considered going directly to other industries that would benefit from those services. I knew a little bit about real estate from a previous job selling model homes and thought, "Why not pitch SCR's services to real estate agents, mortgage lenders, banks, and title companies?"

For this new market, we created high-end newsletters for agents in each of these industries and then allowed them to add their personal information to the materials, which were then sent to their mailing lists automatically. Eventually, we sold the personalized newsletters locally and nationally to real estate agents. In addition to real estate, we had the opportunity to help a few colleges use the same process to recruit students, which was a value add for Josten's.

Although I discovered a few markets before the SCR sale, if I had presented these differently, I could have *increased* value for us. SCR had a hospitality market so other natural synergies might have existed with a hotel chain interested in marketing to brides for wedding receptions. That may have gotten the interest of a mail house or ad agency that helped hotels market by reaching brides and marketing reception services to them. The buyer could have also leveraged direct mail services, giving brides who booked events at the hotel mailing services for invites. This scenario would have been a win-win-win for the buyer, SCR, and the customer.

## BECOME AN INDUSTRY EXPERT, NOT A GENERALIST

Going after markets, or similar types of clients who would benefit from what you already do well, allows you to become an industry expert instead of generalist. It also provides the potential for you to sell more products in more markets that are adjacent to the products you already sell and markets you already enjoy.

Once you establish yourself as an industry expert, you'll generate referrals not only among clients, but among others who want access to your clients. Expanding markets and doing more of what you already do within specific industries will make you more attractive to prospective buyers.

When I sold Alternatives, my advisor and I essentially asked the buyer what he would pay for Alternatives. That was the start and the end of our negotiation. Had I known better, I would have leveraged our markets to drive the value up rather than having the price driven by the buyer.

Not only should an advisor help find potential buyers, but he or she should also help you capitalize on your synergies; an advisor should know when the buyer is giving you the runaround and know when to drive negotiation points, which we'll talk about in Chapter 6. Your responsibility as the seller, of course, is to know how to find the right advisor *and* ask the right questions of the buyer.

## THINK LIKE AMAZON

To expand your list of potential buyers, ask yourself, "What else might my current clients buy?" The following questions can jumpstart this process:

→ Who are my customers and what do they currently buy from my company?

→ Do I have groups of similar companies in the same industry?

→ Can I sell the same types of products and services to adjacent markets?

→ What do my clients need and what would they buy that I don't produce now?

User experience is key. Anything that can make your buyers' lives easier or make your customers' experience more seamless is a selling point. Just look at Amazon. People use Amazon because the experience is easy. You can watch a movie, buy clothes, fill your Kindle, and buy your groceries all in one place.

When it comes to adding services and marketing your company, think like Amazon. Think about ways to expand the buyer's wallet share with your company. Sometimes this means adding products or services like we just talked about. Sometimes it means acquiring or expanding your services into new markets.

## FOR THE BEST OUTCOME, THINK LIKE A BUYER

Presenting your business in a way that's attractive to select buyers starts with thinking like your ideal buyers. What are they looking for? What else do they want to give their clients? What will they want that you have? What will make you more attractive to them?

Returning to the spoon test, your buyer is the restaurant and your business is the spoon. You have to understand everything the buyer wants in order to show him or her how the spoon isn't just one more thing to eat with. It has a specific purpose that will enhance certain elements of the buyer's business.

## UNDERSTAND WHAT THE BUYER IS LOOKING FOR

To know your buyer, you need to know which areas of your business the buyer is looking at. Some buyers will look to add revenue. Others will be more concerned with your gross margin, net profits, or ROI.

A public company, for example, may trade at a higher multiple of earnings than they are buying yours for. If this type of buyer buys your company for say, one times revenue and trades at three times, they would be better off. This could essentially allow the buyer to more than double the value. Therefore, when this type of buyer looks at companies to buy, he or she may be less concerned with your valuation if they can use your revenue earnings using their higher multiple. This can work to the seller's advantage if the seller is aware of the buyer's situation. A seller who doesn't have a clue about the buyer's situation may fail to understand the possibility of negotiating a higher price.

> **NO REGRETS TIP**
> A seller who doesn't have a clue about the buyer's situation may fail to understand the possibility of negotiating a higher price.

A public company could look at how your business helps theirs just like a private buyer will, but it also will consider the market and how your company will impact their stock price when connected to theirs.

Some buyers will be more interested in a seller's potential to capture more market share than they are in the seller's revenue. This type of buyer often looks for sellers that can help them expand into other vertical markets, which are a unique grouping of clients in the same industry. This would allow them to dominate that market and place them in a leadership position to charge more, or easily sell in new products and/or services, which could increase their profits.

Other buyers may look for other differentiators. They'll want to acquire companies that will make them stand out within their market and allow them to expand into other markets. These are synergistic buyers who will often pay more for your company than other types of buyers will.

## FILL THE GAP: ADD ADDITIONAL VALUE

In previous chapters we talked about valuation and how the value a buyer places on a business is often less than what the seller hopes to get for the sale. That creates a gap that needs to be filled. You fill this gap by creating additional value for the buyer, which creates leverage for you.

SCR could have expanded its product/service offerings before the sale. We worked with real estate agents who wore branded shirts and bought other logoed accessories to advertise their brands. If I had thought about it, we could have expanded our search of buyers to include marketing companies that sold ad specialties or apparel. We could have also looked at signage companies or property photographers. We might have convinced these companies that they could have expanded their current product/service revenue by acquiring SCR for our profits and the ability to sell their products to our clients and vice versa.

Before selling Alternatives, I knew many of my clients could have benefited from apparel printing such as uniforms. If I had developed relationships with apparel companies that allowed a buyer to *immediately* do business with those companies, I could have closed that gap and Alternatives might have been more attractive to that type of buyer. This was an oversight on my part.

## DO IT RIGHT THE FIRST TIME

With the Range sale, I thought about adding value before the sale. I knew that if I didn't want to sell to another printer, which was clear in my exit strategy, I'd have to create some synergies for a different type of buyer. Because I wanted a buyer that wouldn't dissolve the manufacturing side of Range but who would offer a good selling price, I had to expand my idea of who I thought a potential buyer might be. Instead of just looking at companies in our industry, I thought, okay, what if I look at marketing companies? What would a marketing company also be interested in?

Before I sold Range, I thought about it from my *clients'* perspective, which helped us position the company in the best light to the buyer. When I bought Range, it was 100 percent paper-based marketing materials. I knew some of our customers would need electronic marketing and fulfillment to market their brands, so I expanded our offering to provide that for our clients, opening a huge market for Range and its potential buyer.

Because some buyers cannot make the leap between what the clients want and how the seller's company might meet that need in the future, the seller needs to fill that gap for the buyer. With Range, I had a unique vertical in the financial market. Even though at the time of the sale that element of Range was a relatively small part of the overall revenue, the buyer fell in love with the idea of expanding its presence into our vertical markets. They also loved that they could use some of Range's existing infrastructure to insource some work, thereby increasing profits, which is a huge selling point. It's amazing how painting a picture of what your company can do and where it can go works potential buyers into a buying frenzy.

---

> Because some buyers cannot make the leap between what the clients want and how the seller's company might meet that need in the future, the seller needs to fill that gap for the buyer.

---

## DEVELOP A MARKETING TEASER

Now that you've looked at what your market opportunities may be, it's time to mirror the needs of your buyers to your company. A teaser is a vanilla overview of your company that showcases the key differentiators, lists the high-level markets you serve, and shows the location in terms of central, east, west, north, and south without going in to exact address, details of clients, or disclosing who your company is. You should call out differentiators that show how a buyer might capitalize on your clients or markets and how you'll add value to the potential buyers you've identified. This is the time to work with your A-Team to develop a marketing teaser to send potential buyers.

Your marketing teaser is your first marketing piece that goes to your broader list of prospects. It should solicit and encourage potential buyers to ask for more information about your company. These teasers are designed to get potential buyers thinking, "Wow, this company could be a great fit for us. How do I learn more about them?"

## VET INTERESTED BUYERS

After potential buyers respond to your marketing teaser, you have to vet them to see if they would be an appropriate buyer for your company. Primarily, you have to see if the buyer aligns with your exit plan and decide whether you want to expose your business to them. If the buyer is located on the other side of the world and one of your exit strategy wont's was "we will not relocate the business," there's no reason to pursue that buyer.

Cross-checking the buyer against your exit strategy will stop you from spending time with a buyer that is an unrealistic fit for your company. A big regret would be to go forward and spend time with a buyer you have *not* researched only to get an LOI, which means they'd like to purchase your company, and find out they are not a fit or don't have the funds to follow through on the sale.

## INVESTIGATE POTENTIAL BUYERS

There are many ways to investigate potential buyers who have responded to your marketing teaser. I generally use two methods. First, I look at how the buyer markets itself. I visit its website, and check social media channels, Google alerts, and Better Business Bureau reviews. Then, I look at the buyer's credit report.

## LOOK AT HOW THE BUYER MARKETS ITSELF

Understanding how a potential buyer markets itself shows how you can pitch your company to complement the buyer. For example, when I presented Range to Deluxe, I presented Range as a marketing communications company that sold to small businesses. Why? Because that's how Deluxe marketed its services. However, unlike Deluxe, Range sold its products to *large* branded networks such as Mary Kay and Berkshire Hathaway Home Services that had thousands of independent small businesses under those brands. By understanding how Deluxe marketed itself and quickly showing Deluxe that both companies serviced and sold to small businesses, we were able to pitch Deluxe on our similarities and how they added value to both companies.

Remember, it's not the buyer's job to say, "What about these synergies? We should pay you for these." The buyer's job is to hand you a black-and-white valuation and get the best deal for them. They will only address the value of your synergies if you raise them.

## CHECK THE BUYER'S CREDIT REPORT

While you're looking at how the buyer markets itself, also look at the company's credit report. Sometimes sellers fail to do this, especially if they're looking at a large, public company, but the buyer's credit standing can have a huge impact on negotiations. A company that is in poor standing or has poor earnings could negatively affect the return of your earnout. You'll want to know this well before going to close because after closing you won't have the control or leverage to change your earnout.

Technology makes this investigative work easy. Look at the buyer's website, LinkedIn, and Facebook profiles for information about marketing. For credit scores, do a credit check through Dunn and Bradstreet or other credit services. Create Google Alerts for the company, which will send immediate news updates about the buyer to your email, and gather information about the company from any other resource you can think of.

## DEVELOP AN OFFERING MEMORANDUM

After vetting the potential buyers who responded to your marketing teaser, you will be ready to send the ones you think are a good fit what is known as an offering memorandum. An offering memorandum essentially serves as your company resume. This memo *must* highlight the things about your company that will be attractive to a buyer.

As the saying goes, you only have one chance to create a first impression. Don't waste that opportunity by producing a generic memo that looks the same to every potential buyer. Even if you're not 100 percent sure if the buyer is a perfect fit, position your company in the best light for that buyer and you can decline an LOI later. Use the information you've gathered about the company, particularly how they market themselves and what you might do for them, to customize each memo.

With the Range sale, I worked with my A-Team to customize each page of every offering memorandum to the potential buyer in a way that looked like Range already existed within that company. If the company was interested in the marketing side of Range, I showed how our existing platforms or clients would expand their brand or save them money once they were insourced.

With the Range sale, I was so determined to package each memo creatively and specifically to each potential buyer that I developed an eye-catching confidential delivery box instead of sending the memos to buyers in traditional FedEx boxes.

As I mentioned before, I learned as much about the buyer as I could before sending an offering memo. Deluxe's growth strategy was easy to find because it is a public company, so the information was available for anyone to research. It was during this research that I discovered Deluxe was in a transformation period and was moving from selling checks and business operating materials to helping small businesses grow by offering marketing materials, website development, SEO services, apparel, ad specialties, and print services. That's how I knew to pitch Range as already working with small businesses.

## SIX THINGS THAT MUST GO IN THE MEMO

As I mentioned earlier, both you and your advisor should be a part of developing the offering memo. You know your company best, and your advisor knows how to present information about your company in the most compelling way.

Regardless of how you pitch your company in the memo, it should include the following six items:

### 1. Name

This should include your company's corporate name as well as how you're known in the market (so the buyer can find you in all searches), your location, and why your location might be unique for the seller. Maybe it's close to a certain type of worker, is next to a core client group, or offers reduced costs. If location is not important—if it's just a lease that you fell into and your exit strategy states that you're okay with moving, or the buyer has similar, nearby locations—state that your current location is a great opportunity to consolidate for cost savings.

## 2. History

This should include when and why you started your company. It's critical to include what need or void you set out to fill. This is a brief overview of what you have accomplished. Be proud of it and enjoy writing this section of the memo.

## 3. Industry

What industry are you in? Manufacturing? Marketing? Technology? While it may sometimes seem obvious, defining your business could be a huge selling point that might otherwise get overlooked.

Once at a conference, the CEO of Harley Davidson Motorcycles asked the attendees which business we thought he was in. A few audience members laughed and said, "That's easy, you're in the motorcycle business." Someone else yelled that he was in the recreation/transportation business. The CEO paused and then said, "No, we are in the lifestyle business."

It turns out that Harley sold more logoed products than they did new motorcycles. See how the industry you're actually in can change how a potential buyer sees your company? Make sure to clearly define your industry for yourself before you pitch your business to someone else.

## 4. Market

It's critical to address who you serve and why. What do you do better than others in your market? How do you go to market and how do you make money?

This is a great place to showcase your marketing materials. This document needs to create excitement and show how you can add value to the buyer. It needs to get that buyer asking questions about your company. It needs to motivate the reader to say, "I need to meet this seller in person."

This is the place in your resume that sets you apart and gets you that interview!

## 5. Customers

While you don't need to put the names of your customers here yet, you do need to describe what your customers look like. What types of customers do you have? How many do you have? What about these customers is valuable to the buyer? Are they long-term clients? Do you have contracts? Do you have a unique product or service that your competitors don't have?

### 6. Numbers

This is the references section of your resume. It supports every claim you've made up to this point. If you say you're experiencing a growth curve, then you present your supporting numbers here. If your last two years were high growth, but three years ago you experienced a decline, you might show the last two years as well as a forecast you expect to achieve for the next two years.

Although a lot of information goes into your offering memo, to get the most interested buyers you and your advisors should spend a great deal of time crafting each one.

It's important to note here that you'll likely send your offering memos in a tiered format. The first tier includes the buyers you're most interested in selling to. If the first tier of memos comes back with no response, send your tier-two memos and so on. Keep this in mind as you vet potential buyers and keep the ones you're most interested in at the top of the pile.

**NO REGRETS JOURNAL ENTRY**

**BUILD YOUR PROSPECT LIST.** Who would be your dream buyer? Complete a company spoon test and refine this list annually.

_____

_____

_____

_____

_____

_____

_____

**START THINKING ABOUT YOUR MARKETING TEASER.** What are your company's strengths today? What would catch a buyer's eye? Do this year over year. Do your answers change? Do you need to do things differently from year to year to attract the right buyer?

_____

_____

_____

_____

_____

_____

_____

**THINK ABOUT YOUR COMPANY'S ACCOMPLISHMENTS.**
Which accomplishments would you list for your company if you were
building a resume for it? What do you need to adjust, build, or buy to
improve your company?

_____

_____

_____

_____

_____

_____

_____

_____

_____

_____

_____

_____

_____

_____

_____

Find a Buyer

# SECTION 3

# CLOSE THE DEAL

# CHAPTER 6

➡

# MASTER THE
# SALES PROCESS

*"In modern business, it is not the crook who
is to be feared most, it is the honest man
who doesn't know what he is doing."*

— WILLIAM WORDSWORTH

BY THE TIME THE ALTERNATIVES SALE got to the sales process, I'd already made *numerous* mistakes. I didn't have an exit strategy, I hadn't picked the right A-Team, I didn't know much about valuation or how to make Alternatives more attractive to potential buyers and, instead of *looking* for buyers, I accepted the first buyer that showed any interest.

Then I made another mistake: I failed to understand the sales process and how it would affect my outcome after the sale. For starters, I didn't understand how the buyer marketed itself and therefore didn't fully understand how Alternatives could fit into the buyer's business model.

Alternatives brokered out its print production to several different printers. If we really looked at the buyer, which printed in-house, and saw that bringing Alternatives printing in-house would have saved the buyer a lot of money, I could have negotiated a better deal for the Alternatives sale. Had I been paying attention and done more research, I could have negotiated a better deal on a second point: The buyer planned to consolidate our fulfillment. That was a huge cost savings to the buyer that I missed. I may also have chosen not to sell based on the future potential consolidation plans. The problem was, I didn't know what to look for during the sales process that would have saved me from heartache later.

> ### NO REGRETS TIP
> Know what to look for to save yourself
> from heartache later.

## WHAT IS THE SALES PROCESS?

The sales process is what happens after potential buyers respond to the offering memorandums. You've told them what you have to offer, they're interested, and now it's time to get to know them so you can potentially get to a stage where they present you with a LOI.

Specifically, the sales process involves vetting potential buyers, then deciding which potential buyer gets more information from you, then moving them to the point of presenting a LOI. After receiving an LOI, you will have to negotiate LOI terms, continue impressing the potential buyer during due diligence, work with the buyer to create a transition plan, and complete the closing papers.

## WHEN THE BUYER RESPONDS

Waiting for responses to the offering memorandum can be nerve-wracking. What if no one responds? What if no one likes your company? Why is this taking so long?

When I first started selling companies, I asked myself those questions frequently after sending out offering memorandums. However, sellers who do their research, work with a good A-Team, and position their company well within the market seldom go without getting a single LOI.

Response time from a buyer can take weeks to a month. Sometimes they say no, not now. Maybe the timing isn't good or they don't feel your company is a good fit. Sometimes they are very interested and want to meet you right away. An interested buyer will want to meet you, see your company, discuss your thoughts about the sale, and tell you their thoughts about what the sale means to them. This is when the selling *really* starts. It's time to sell yourself!

This process is a little like dating. You need to court your buyers, show you know something about their company, and explain how your company will complement theirs.

Every meeting, call, or presentation you have with your buyer either enhances or detracts from the possibility of getting an LOI, or a second date. If the buyer feels you are not being straightforward with your communications, it will raise doubts. If you can't get the documents they ask for quickly, this will cause doubts. If they meet you and you're impersonal, or communicate in a way that's off-putting, they may lose interest. They may also raise an eyebrow if you—the seller—don't want to stay after the sale unless you share the reasons upfront. Remember, if you don't stay, the buyer will need to figure out whether their current executive team has the capacity to take over management.

---

> Sellers who do their research, work
> with a good A-Team, and position their
> company well within the market seldom
> go without getting a single LOI.

---

## COURTING YOUR BUYER: THE FIRST DATE

The first meeting with any potential buyer is like a blind date. You know a little bit about each other from some basic communications, Facebook research, and Google searches, but this is your first face-to-face. This is your opportunity to sell yourself and your company. This is selling at its highest level.

I first met the Deluxe team for lunch. It was a basic meet-and-greet to test compatibility and interest level. This initial meeting should be held in a neutral location such as a coffee shop or restaurant rather than at either company headquarters. Like a first date, this meeting will have everyone on their best behavior and the conversation should be general get-to-know-you stuff. Where are they from? Do they have a family? What do they do in their free time? The buyer and seller need to get to know each other as people to see what doing business together might look like and what their communications styles are like. No matter how sweet the deal is, if the buyer and seller don't get along, it should not happen.

I always tell sellers to dress for this meeting like they would if they were interviewing for a job with that company. If you're in manufacturing and that means you'd wear khakis, wear khakis. If it means a three-piece suit, wear a three-piece suit. You want to be yourself while also accurately presenting your company.

### Leave Your Defenses at Home

What you *don't* want to do during this meeting, or at any point during the sales process, is get your defenses up. Buyers often ask questions that sellers find insulting. Remember, buyers are looking at companies in very black-and-white terms. They may question why Pam is paid $100,000 when the average salary for someone in her position is $60,000. They don't know how many late nights Pam worked when you first started, or how many jobs she really did before you were able to hire additional staff. They are looking at Pam and your operations from a black-and-white standpoint. This viewpoint often irritates sellers, but this is another stage of selling where a good advisor is really useful. The advisor will stick to the facts, which will help keep your defenses down.

## THE SECOND DATE: THE BUYER VISITS YOU

Following the first meeting, if you and your potential buyer are still interested, the buyer will ask to see your company. This is fun, but it can also be unnerving. I tell all sellers to treat the buyer's visit like they would a prospective client. You need to showcase your company in the best light and present the company in a way that highlights the services and products the buyer might be interested in.

At this stage, there's no point in causing panic among employees by telling them what's happening. I know this can be difficult—you want to be straight with your employees—but there's no reason to set off the alarm bells when you've just started the sales process. One company visit certainly doesn't guarantee a sale, so don't let your employees worry. Worry just borrows trouble before its time.

---

One company visit certainly doesn't guarantee a sale, so don't let your employees worry. Worry just borrows trouble before its time.

---

Before touring potential buyers around your company, meet in a private conference room, give a preview of what they will see, share any necessary, confidential facts, and ask that they hold all questions until the end of the visit. This allows them to fully see operations and prevents employees from hearing questions that may tip them off to the sale.

Know that during this visit, you'll naturally default to your own skill-set. If you're a natural salesperson, you'll sell. If you're good with numbers, you'll highlight analytics. If you're great at operations, you'll talk about operations. Your advisor should make sure other benefits are discussed. He or she will also step in when the buyer asks questions that you may find insulting. Remember, the advisor's job is to be the intermediary. Without an advisor, the sales process can become an emotional free-for-all.

### THE THIRD DATE: VISIT THE BUYER

When additional questions come up after the onsite visit, I recommend that the seller visit the buyer at their headquarters. I did this with the Range sale. I wanted to know what working for Deluxe would be like for my employees. There's no better way to do this than an onsite visit. Just like buyers get a sense of your culture the minute they walk into your company, you get insights into buyers' cultures the minute you visit them. Culture is a huge smell test. Do the employees look happy? Can you see your employees working with them? Is the buyer relaxed or formal with them? Would you fit in?

Onsite visits allow the buyer and seller to present themselves to each other. When Deluxe visited Range for our second date, I showed them how they could benefit beyond revenue and profits. Deluxe showed me the additional value they could bring to our clients and employees beyond just the purchase price. Essentially, we showed each other how we might act as partners.

---

## Just like buyers get a sense of your culture the minute they walk into your company, you get insights into the buyers' cultures the minute you visit them.

---

While everyone is playing poker—both the buyer and seller want a deal that will most benefit them—getting to know the people within the buyer's company tells the seller a lot. For example, when I sold Alternatives, I visited the buyer over Christmas break. Instead of meeting with the president, which is who I would work for when Alternatives became a part of the buyer's company, I met with the CEO. Meeting with the president would have spoken volumes as to what would happen when I started working with him and whether it would be a good fit. Unfortunately, *I was too naive* to think of things in those terms. Needless to say, it was not a good fit and I didn't stay on long after the sale. That being said, never burn a bridge, a point I'll discuss later in the book. If handled correctly, every cloud has a silver lining.

Keep in mind that you'll likely play this dating game with several buyers at once. Think of yourself as one of the stars on *The Bachelor* or *The Bachelorette*. You're dating several people, eliminating the ones that don't work, and moving forward with those that might.

### THE WAITING GAME

After the get-to-know-you phase, your potential buyers will either exit and date someone else, or ask to go exclusive by presenting a LOI.

Every advisor communicates differently with buyers. Some advisors like to present sales price ranges so buyers submit blind LOIs. In this case, the advisor may tell the buyer the company is valued at between $5 and $7 million. They do this in hopes of driving up the bids. You can also tell the buyer exactly what you're looking for. This will prevent headaches and extra work during the due diligence process.

Just like when you're awaiting responses to your memo, waiting for an LOI is a patience game. Don't act too eager. It can take six to twelve months for an acquisition to complete, so take a deep breath and resist the temptation to jump at the first offer.

Wait for all LOIs to come in and then make a decision that falls in line with your exit strategy. Remember, you're not engaged yet, but in most cases, an LOI will come with an exclusive clause, meaning that once you accept, you need to discontinue marketing to others while working through due diligence. Be very careful about who you share this stage with because that person or people could say something that could completely derail all the work you did, or they could tell staff and distract them from doing their jobs.

It's best to wait until you reach due diligence, which occurs after the LOIs come in, before introducing additional team members or company leaders to the sale. Premature announcements create worry, and if you don't get an acceptable LOI, then you create worry for no reason.

## THE ENGAGEMENT: THE PRESENTATION OF THE LOI

You've dated a few people now and a few of your dates are interested in dating you exclusively, so they put in an LOI.

Technically, an LOI can come in at any point during the sales process. Maybe you send a memo to one company who tried to buy a company like yours, but the deal fell through. That type of buyer instantly knows they want to buy, so they may want to send an LOI that week to try to lock you up. This can be an ideal scenario; however, the down side is this may be the first offer and other interested buyers may be working through the selling discovery process before presenting an LOI. Your advisor should set a time limit for when all LOIs are due. They should share when one LOI is on the table with other interested buyers so those potential buyers know to get their LOIs in by a certain date.

Most LOIs are one- to two-page letters on the buyer's letterhead stating the buyer's desire to buy your company. The offers will come to your advisor, who will work hard to make sure the LOI falls in line with your exit strategy. The buyer usually specifies a deadline for a response, which can be negotiated if the seller feels it isn't enough time to receive the other pending LOIs.

## PREPARE FOR AN EMOTIONAL ROLLER COASTER

Regardless of how or when you receive your LOIs or how many you receive, getting an LOI is an emotional roller coaster. First there's the up, or the excitement of knowing someone finds your company valuable. They want what you've built and they'll pay for it. What could be more gratifying? This feeling lasts a few minutes before the doubt sets in. What if this buyer is the wrong one? How will you know if they're the right fit for your employees?

I remember the excitement of receiving the LOI for Alternatives like it was yesterday. My wife, Sandi, and I had just returned from a Caribbean cruise and were waiting our turn to disembark the ship in Miami. I had a voice message from my advisor. He asked me to call him back and then said, "I got the LOI!"

We didn't have smartphones yet, so I couldn't get an email of the letter, but I called my advisor back immediately. He read the offer, which I could hardly focus on because I was so excited. Hearing the actual number a buyer is willing to pay for your company can be very exciting.

Of all the elements of the sale that have changed for me over the years, the one feeling that hasn't is when I'm handed an LOI. That excitement has never changed. In 2014, when I received the LOI from Deluxe, I felt no different than I did in 1998 when I received the LOI from Merrill. The only difference was that in 2014, I received my LOI on my iPhone in my Minnesota home while looking out the window at a snowstorm. Technology had changed and so had my landscape.

## WHAT TO EXPECT FROM AN LOI

While your advisor will help assess your LOIs, you should generally know what an LOI contains. An LOI states the buyer's intent to purchase your company, the amount the buyer is willing to pay assuming everything you presented and they have reviewed is correct and auditable, how the payments will be made, and the expected closing date. Every piece of the LOI is contingent on the outcome of due diligence and the confirmation of the information you've presented to the buyer.

Specifically, an LOI states the following:

→ Buyer's intent to purchase your company

→ Mutual Confidentiality Nondisclosure Agreement

→ Exclusive right[1]

→ Type of sale: Stock or asset

→ Amount the buyer is willing to pay and how he or she will pay you

→ Due diligence timeline

→ Expected closing date

→ Any other specific terms

While getting an LOI is exciting, the important thing to remember is that an LOI is only an *intention* from the buyer, *not* a commitment to buy. Even when you receive an LOI that you want to move forward with, everything in that LOI is subject to your due diligence process. Depending on the outcome of the due diligence, you could end up with additional negotiations. The LOI is not binding as far as the buyer's offer to buy, and you also have the right to decline if terms are not met and you can ask for a buyer due diligence clause.

## THE LOI: WHERE NEGOTIATION BEGINS

Getting to the LOI stage is the fun part of selling. It's where the negotiations begin. It's also where all the efforts you put into your presale and package to market processes pay off. This is a pivotal moment that will either lead to the high of closing a great sale that falls in line with your exit strategy, or the low of regrets. This is your chance to reflect on your exit strategy and your future plans.

During this process, you need to channel your excitement. There's a whole host of work that has to be done before the deal closes, and it starts with due diligence. You haven't signed over the company yet,

Close the Deal

---

1 Most ask for this so the buyer has control or a guarantee if terms are met. This allows the buyer to take your company off the market while they do their due diligence.

you've just agreed to the terms of the LOI contingent on neither you nor the buyer finding any surprises.

There are a few elements within the LOI that are contractually binding, including confidentiality, the disclosure agreement, and the exclusivity period and deadline for completing the sale by a certain date. In some cases, particularly with bigger deals, the LOI may include a provision requiring the buyer or the seller to pay the due diligence fees if both get close to closing and one backs out of the deal without cause. With smaller sales, particularly if the seller is looking at several LOIs at once, this typically will not be the case.

One key thing many sellers struggle to understand is that once you close on the sale, that's it. You no longer own your business. You're not the decision maker. You won't be able to control or affect the outcome because the business is simply no longer yours.

---

One key thing many sellers struggle to understand is that once you close on the sale, that's it. You no longer own your business.

---

## STRUCTURE YOUR PAYOUT

During LOI negotiations, you will also need to consider your payout. There are many ways to structure your payout, but if you understand the differences and are flexible in how you approach your payout, you may be able to provide more value to the buyer and, ultimately, broker a better deal for yourself, your business, and your employees.

Let's look at how the three basic types of payments can work for the seller:

1. **Earnouts**: Some cash at closing plus an earnout can have the highest payout but come with risks.

2. **Guaranteed payments:** Some cash at closing plus future guaranteed payments can net more than an all-cash deal and have limited risks compared to an earnout.

3. **All cash at closing:** This comes with no upside of future payments or earnout. Typically, this can net the least. It also comes without future risks, which is great if you plan to leave the business or are looking for a very low risk versus reward scenario.

## 1. EARNOUTS

Earnouts can come in a combination of cash and performance payments. Sellers who have had a few rocky years or a higher sale price than the buyer is willing to offer will need an earnout to complete a deal.

With an earnout, the buyer pays less up front with an offer to pay more over time if the company hits certain performance metrics. Earnouts do not include an additional guarantee to pay more unless the seller delivers. These payouts can be very tricky and can end poorly for the seller if the seller does not understand earnout calculations.

With an earnout, the risk for the seller increases when the seller doesn't ask the right questions and doesn't know going into the deal what will happen with staff, revenue, and the other considerations that can affect the seller's ability to meet earnout requirements. The risk to the seller also increases if the seller doesn't vet the buyer and the buyer ends up going under.

Earnouts can be incredibly complicated. When I sold Alternatives, one of my biggest regrets and largest life lesson was delivered with my earnout. When we were negotiating the sale price, the buyer presented a purchase price that was 25 percent higher than I had expected, but it included an earnout component. The deal included 50 percent cash due at closing and then an earnout if we achieved specific performance metrics. So, in this case, the remaining 50 percent of the company plus the upside on the additional 25 percent bonus were tied to my earnout metrics. To achieve the additional payments, I had to meet three metrics that became very difficult to track. They included:

→ Revenue

→ Gross margin

→ Net profit

I felt like I had to jump on one foot, touch my head, wiggle my arm, and hope the moon was in the right alignment just so I could get paid—a pain I caused myself because I hadn't asked the right questions of the buyer and hadn't really understood the terms of my payout. At first these metrics seemed to be easy to track. However, I will share what can affect your payments so you can plan accordingly.

### Earnout Metrics

It's tough to come out with a win-win when an earnout is involved in a sale. While earnouts are used to help bridge the current value the buyer is willing to pay and what the seller believes the actual value is based on synergies, earnouts are complicated and not guaranteed. The more metrics put into place to measure the earnout, the more difficult the earnout is to track. And the more difficult the earnout is to track, the more difficult it can be to receive your payments.

If you're considering an earnout option, you need to understand which parts of the earnout will affect your ability to meet your earnout metrics. These variables include sales growth, gross margin, operating expenses, and net operating income.

### Sales Growth

For the Alternatives sale, the earnout metric was based on sales growth year over year.

Based on the past performance of Alternatives, I thought this would be easy to increase. The sale freed me from worrying about the many components of running a business and the buyer said I was getting new sales resources, so I thought my targets would be a layup. Of course, it wasn't that easy. I had lost control over my sales team, which directly impacted my bottom line.

### Gross Margin/Cost of Goods Sold (COGS)

Gross margin, which is the difference between revenue and cost of goods sold, is a fairly easy metric to understand. Typically, gross margin gets better with volume efficiencies.

You will, however, need to understand how the buyer places costs. Think about costs like buckets and make sure they're going into the right bucket. Make sure costs are placed in relation to products, services, or sales, and that they align with the same assessments the buyer will be using.

Labor expenses as they relate to projects—especially technology in areas such as web portals built for selling your products and services—may be a cost of goods if the client is paying for customization. However, these costs could also be considered an operating expense if the labor is just a way to sell your products and services and is not billable. The difference between the two can greatly affect your gross margin. It does not, however, affect the net operating income overall if accounted correctly.

### Operating Expenses/Sales and General Administration (SGA)

Operating expenses are measured differently, which presents a challenge if you do not know how they will be measured as part of your valuation.

With the Alternatives sale, I thought I'd have more control over operating expenses like I did when I was the owner. As I learned, there ended up being a number of chargebacks, or disputed transactions, and so-called shared services that factored into those expenses. The shared services were essentially a portion of the buyer's expenses, which were transferred to Alternatives after the sale. The theory behind the transfer was that Alternatives would be more efficient and could do more with the economies of scale and the buyer would save costs.

> **NO REGRETS TIP**
> Adjust to having less control. Do not assume that when you sell your company, you will have as much control over operating expenses as you did when you owned it.

Shared services that might impact your sale could include operations, human resources, and finance. I did not have a say in the allocation amount of these expenses, how the individuals were managed, or whether we had the resources to meet the increased need.

The reality was, I received a chargeback of corporate overhead based on my percentage of the revenue versus expenses from the buyer. I needed to maintain the current costs as a ratio for the first two years, and then it could increase as we grew and I could add staff. The problem

Close the Deal

is, if you have revenue increase goals you have to do this with existing staff so you don't go out of the first year's ratios. Again, the assumption that *I made* was that I would be able to scale based again on my ability to leverage the larger company's resources, but this didn't happen.

### Net Operating Income

Generally, it is difficult to control the number that represents your net operating income because it gets confused during amortizations and depreciating schedules.

Because I didn't fully understand metrics when I went into the Alternatives sale, I thought everything looked great. The total compensation was still much higher than if the buyer paid all cash or paid cash plus a set note. I also loved that Merrill was public. I liked the idea of receiving stock options and the ability to buy stock at a discount going forward. However, because I didn't understand these metrics, I placed more risk and netted less cash overall.

Earnouts are not all bad if done correctly. This starts with *completely* understanding how the earnout will be measured and how you as a seller can affect the outcome. In addition to understanding the metrics, you also need to understand the complexity of the earnout because this may impact how payments are structured.

With the Alternatives sale, knowing what I know today would have increased my cash at closing and added a portion of the earnout as guaranteed payments and a staying bonus for key employees. The significant amount of changes that occur during and after a sale require a carrot to keep people on. A staying bonus would have helped me stay the course as I negotiated the earnout and other compensation for key members of staff who ended up leaving.

### Due Diligence and Earnout Factors You Need to Understand

As you are considering earnouts metrics and how they will impact your company, there are a few key things that can drastically affect your future outcomes.

For example, you need to know before agreeing to the deal if the buyer is going to allocate their overhead to you when they buy your company. If you made 10 percent to bottom before the sale, but the added overhead will hit you by 3 percent, you can go back to the buyer and say, "Okay, if you're going to do that, then that 3 percent gets reflected in my earnout."

If the buyer wants to change a few key elements that will impact your ability to hit revenue targets, you want to make sure that impact is reflected in your targets or your earnout payout. If you're not happy with the deal offered, this is your time to say something. Remember, once the sale is done, you can't go back and fix or renegotiate items you decide you don't like.

Specifically, there are five key things that may hinder your ability to manage your company and potentially receive all the payouts stated in the closing documents. These include your clients' tax ramifications, sales/revenue recognition, employee/benefits plan changes, employee reviews and merit increases, and cost-of-living increases.

### Tax Ramifications

When you start negotiating with a buyer, numerous things you may not have thought of will come to light. For small to mid-sized sellers who do not have out-of-state sales offices, this can be a real wakeup call if they broker a deal with a buyer who does. If the buyer has sales offices in other states, you may suddenly have to start collecting tax from customers in those states.

Thankfully, when we sold Range I'd been through several sales and knew to ask about out-of-state sales tax. Because Deluxe is a national company with sales offices in other states, once Deluxe acquired Range, it had to start collecting tax from out-of-state customers who we hadn't previously collected tax from.

If sales tax will affect your customers make sure that when you announce the sale to your customers, you explain how billing will change. Let them know that you've got it handled and you've got a plan to make sure it has the least amount of impact on them as possible. The last thing you want after a sale is a bunch of unhappy customers.

### Sales/Revenue Recognition

Sales/revenue recognition is how you and the seller recognize revenue, and it can have a huge impact on earnouts.

Revenue is affected by a variety of things, including staff and your ability to hire and manage them, which can change after the

Close the Deal

sale. When Alternatives sold, the new management decided that the noncompetes we had in place were null and void and new ones needed to be signed. Because my salespeople didn't like how things were run after the sale, they left. So not only did I lose sales staff, I couldn't hire the new sales team I wanted. I was left with fewer sales and still expected to meet the revenue metrics outlined in my earnout, but that didn't happen. You can avoid this by reviewing agreements during due diligence and working with your A-Team to carefully examine HR and legal documents and how they might affect the offer.

If you and the buyer recognize sales and revenue differently, the buyer may expect you to produce higher revenues later, which will affect your earnout. Or, if you don't know what the buyer is measuring or how they plan to handle certain aspects of the sale, they may actually hinder your ability to hit those earnout numbers.

With Range, I calculated revenue on sales before postage. The buyer recognized revenue *after* postage. I sent a lot of direct mail and the difference in revenue before and after postage was large. This meant that in Deluxe's view, Range's revenues were higher than previously thought. In my view, the recognized revenue would have been lower, but in this case, I would have benefited from an earnout.

### Employee/Benefits Plan Changes

If your earnout is based on bottom-line profits and the buyer has a better benefits plan, it can also affect your earnout; if it costs more, it will cause your overall costs to increase.

When I sold Alternatives, the buyer's benefits plan was much better. This was a benefit to our employees, which was great, but we got charged more for the plan, which affected my ability to meet my earnout net operating numbers. I was naïve and didn't realize this until later, of course.

The Range sale worked out much better. The buyer's benefits package was better and much cheaper than Range's. Part of this had to do with federal changes to healthcare laws and the difference between how healthcare is offered in a small company versus a large company. Since I'd been through numerous sales, I knew to ask about benefits packages so I could determine how they would affect our performance.

### Employee Reviews and Merit Increases

Before selling, you may have given raises based on how a person helped you grow the company or the extra effort they gave. When you become a part of another company, your employees' salaries and pay grades will be based on whatever model that company chooses to use. If those pay grades are higher, that increases your costs and affects your earnout.

With the Range sale, we knew Deluxe would offer employees working under forty hours a week benefits whereas we only offered benefits to traditionally classified full-time employees. Because we knew this before the sale, we were able to factor this into our negotiations.

### Cost-of-Living Increases

Larger companies tend to set cost-of-living increases not to exceed a percent of a total pool. If the total payout for your team can only be 2.5 percent, that means that if one of your employees has a higher review, you can only give them a small increase over the 2.5. If you give them a 3 percent increase you will need to give another employee a 2 percent increase, assuming he or she makes similar amounts. If you're giving a higher-paid employee a 3 percent increase and a lower paid-person a 2 percent increase, you may have to give less to the higher or less to the lower so the total pool does not exceed the 2.5 percent total allowed.

This could be a positive or negative scenario based on the type of increase your employees are accustomed to receiving. If this decreases, you could lose some key people, which of course threatens to impact the overall performance needed to hit your earnout.

### Clients'/Vendors' Payables and Receivables Terms

If you integrate a new payment system, which is common after a sale, you can't promise you will pay someone differently than everyone else. You also can't allow one customer to stretch out payments when the new company has specific terms. Their policy may be to turn them over to a collections agency even if you know that the customer is good for it; they may not want to hold the receivable open.

Close the Deal

### Hiring Support Staff

Unlike before the sale, after the sale you'll likely have a hiring budget. Oftentimes, these budgets mean you can't hire someone until you hit a certain revenue that will support the costs related to the hire. This, of course, affects your ability to meet your targets.

> ## NO REGRETS TIP
> Understand the post-sale hiring process. After the sale you'll likely have a hiring budget. Oftentimes, these budgets mean you can't hire someone until you hit a certain revenue that will support the costs related to the hire. This, of course, affects your ability to meet your targets.

### Hiring New Sales Staff

Hiring new sales staff is a critical growth component. You may need to increase existing sales quotas, but the buyer may have you wait until you have the additional margin to cover a new role. Before the sale, of course, if you needed new staff you might say, "I'm okay making less for this month, quarter, or year as an investment in growth." After the sale, you can't do that anymore.

### Shared Services

These include common departments you may share with the buyer such as finance, IT, manufacturing, and purchasing. The buyer may want you to use their existing staff and reposition or remove your current staff.

### Locations

The buyer may want you to move into their building or move a service or function such as a warehouse or manufacturing facility. They may ask you to have staff work from home. Regardless, the way you did business before the sale and after will be different. Make sure you know where the buyer is headed with location so you can be prepared to limit the client disruptions this could cause.

### Technology

You should know the overall plan for investing in technology platforms and equipment. You may need to match the buyer's system. It's important to know this and where those costs will fall.

## 2. CASH WITH GUARANTEED PAYMENTS

Fixed-price payments typically have a smaller down payment and then include guaranteed payments for the remaining amount over a specific period.

With this payout option, if the seller is willing to take a percent of the sale price at closing, the buyer may pay the balance over a certain agreed-upon period of time such as five years. This type of purchase should also include an additional interest rate on the balance owed to the seller. This allows the buyer to have the company's cash flow to pay the seller versus paying it all at closing. In essence, the buyer buys the company for a percent of its valuation, and therefore may be willing to pay a larger overall purchase price rather than paying cash at closing.

Be careful to vet the stability of the buyer and get a personal guarantee. In the event the buyer runs your company into the ground, this ensures they can make the payments.

Guaranteed cash payments can result in a larger payout. For example, say that going into a sale you believe you have a potential new client contract. If that's the case, you can negotiate a separate payout based on when the contract is signed. As soon as it is, you get a payout. Once a guaranteed cash payment is signed, you receive an additional guaranteed payment on any new sales you may have had in the pipeline prior to closing.

Putting less money down and personally guaranteeing the balance owed can be a win-win for both the buyer and seller. The seller gets more money and the buyer has to come up with less up front, allowing them to invest more capital if needed. The key to this type of deal is the credit worthiness of the buyer and the collateral (your guarantee to get paid) that the buyer puts forward. You don't want the buyer to only use the company as collateral because if they run it into the ground

Close the Deal

and quit paying, you end up getting a broken company that you then have to jump back into and run.

From a seller's perspective, this method can result in a better price. And, as long as you're flexible with payout options, it may also mean that you get more value for your business.

The downside for the seller is that they have to trust the buyer will make good on the additional payments. Buyers interested in this type of payout may have less cash available or feel the need to further invest additional cash in the business. To compensate for paying a lower cash price, they will pay more over time.

When I bought Range, my goal was to rebuild Range for growth and then sell it. For years before I got involved with Range, sales were static or had slightly declined. Before buying Range, I looked at the seller's valuation and their desired sales number and placed that against the current profits and cash flow. To me, Range appeared to be off in terms of the sellers' value of it and mine.

I continued using the valuation methods built by the seller's accounting firm, which looked at the average of monthly results at the close of each month. This method was almost like buying stocks on the open market. So, if March was a great month, and April was terrible, value would swing considerably from month to month based on the previous month's results.

Once I started talking to the sellers, who had already refused one buyer because they didn't want the company dissolved, I realized that the amount of cash at closing was not as important to them as ongoing cash flow and other benefits, such as keeping Range intact. Because the sellers had built and worked in the company for more than thirty-five years and Range was a second-generation company, the sale had a lot of emotional impact. Money certainly wasn't the most important thing to the sellers, which affected valuation.

The sellers wanted out, and the market timing was not in their favor. When a seller goes through this process with a buyer, he or she needs to understand the buyer's growth plans to see if the company will have the ability to grow and pay future payments. Once I understood why the sellers didn't need all cash at close, I asked if they'd be willing to receive payments over time. This conversation opened the door for me to revisit what I was willing to pay for the company and what I felt I could build the company into within a short period of time.

As value and prices continued to decline at Range, I began to understand what the value of Range could be if I repositioned it as a marketing company. I felt comfortable that with Range under my direction, we could quickly spin off the additional cash flow needed to make a profit and make the needed payments to the sellers. This purchase scenario ended up being the perfect match for both of us.

We landed on structuring a fixed price with a small down payment and a long-term guaranteed note at current market interest rates. This allowed me to buy the company with little cash down and make the initial investments needed to quickly grow and add revenue.

## 3. ALL CASH AT CLOSING

When we sold Range's marketing services to Deluxe, we agreed on a cash deal. That meant we received 90 percent of the agreed-upon amount at closing with only 10 percent held back for a short period of time. This was to protect the buyer until we confirmed our inventory amounts, that our contracts would transfer, and that all our statements about the company were true. It also confirmed a guaranteed payment to us after all was verified.

### Sign the LOI

Once you have reviewed all the offers and negotiated the terms, the deal is far from done. Next, you have to work through the due diligence process. This is another instance where deals can fall apart. As the buyer learns more about the seller's company, they may find out there are additional costs to consider. Maybe the building needs a new roof or the technology is outdated or won't interface with theirs. Each time one of these costs surfaces, it presents another negotiation. Your LOI terms can go out the window and you may have to start over negotiating if things are uncovered that were not disclosed. It is really important to have your documents in order during the marketing and sales process. If you don't, the deal could blow up during due diligence.

### Start Due Diligence

The due diligence process is all about asking good questions so the seller doesn't leave the sale filled with regrets. It's about comparing what the buyer wants to what the seller expects, weighing the positives and negatives of both, and using them to create leverage for the future negotiation.

---

> The due diligence process is all about asking good questions so the seller doesn't leave the sale filled with regrets.

---

When you go through due diligence, you'll frequently meet with the buyer to ensure that you've sent the documents the buyer wants. Your A-Team will help guide you through negotiations and help you understand which negotiations to accept and which to table. You should discuss these things early on so you don't decide something is a deal breaker when the sale is as far as the transition plan or, even worse, after the sale closes and you can't do anything about it. Again, this should all be documented in your exit strategy so you and your advisor have a clear picture of what you want and don't want from the start.

### Gather Your I-Team

The first step in due diligence is to gather your internal leadership team, who I call the I-Team.

This group of key employees will help gather the information the buyer needs during due diligence. Usually, this team includes department heads and your key leaders. Who you include will depend on the type of sale and the buyer's interest in your company. If the buyers are particularly interested in your technologies, they'll need time with your tech team. If they're interested in operations, prepare for your operations/manufacturing leader to spend some time with them.

Once you pick your team, sit down with them. Let them know the company is for sale and that you might have a buyer. Be sure to explain your reasons for the sale and why you think it's the best move for those staff members as well as the company. Then, make sure you have a plan to give your I-Team an incentive to help prepare the sale. This gives them a vested interest to help you get the deal done. These key people will do a lot of extra work to help move the sale forward. The work you did during the presale process will help, but this internal team will gather additional documents and meet with the buyer in addition to their own duties. Explain what bonus you'll offer each after the sale.

When you gather your core leaders and explain your reasons for selling, be prepared for a litany of questions. Put yourself in their shoes, think of questions they might ask, and prepare your answers in advance. Key on their minds will be, "What's going to happen to my job?" If the team you gather is large, announce that you're considering a sale to the whole group so they all get the news from you. This will avoid hurt feelings. If you have only a couple of key leaders, meet with them individually, back to back. Do this based on tenure, role within the company, and how you feel each person will react.

If you do not work through due diligence with your A-Team and I-Team, you will leave money on the table and sign a deal that leads to regrets. In many cases, you may end up leaving with a much lower payout than you anticipated. Due diligence is your time to negotiate. Make sure you do it well.

## Keep the Sale on a Need-to-Know Basis

While your I-Team is critical to making the deal happen, do not share the potential sale with your entire staff. The sale is far from over. A premature announcement may upset people for no reason, disrupt workflow, and cause certain staff to leave. Due diligence can be disruptive and hard on those key team members, but you still want them focused on clients, not on the sales process.

Once, when I was looking to acquire a company, the owner announced the sale before we finished due diligence. I asked him not to do this. It's not uncommon for buyers to find things during due diligence that prevent them from going through with the sale. This particular seller felt he needed total transparency with his staff, so he decided to announce the sale before it happened.

When he made the announcement, his office became a revolving door. Employees wanted to know what would happen and what their new role would look like. Of course, he couldn't answer any of these questions because the deal wasn't done. This owner brought on so much unnecessary stress that he lost a few key members of this team as well as a few customers. His employees set their sights on finding new jobs and spent time discussing what-ifs with each other instead of focusing on customers. This chaos is exactly why you don't want to announce early to a large group.

After I completed the due diligence for this sale, I found some accounting errors that initially resulted in having to revise the LOI purchase price. Ultimately, the deal fell through and the seller ended up losing a couple of key employees and customers from announcing the sale prematurely.

### Manage Your Due Diligence Team

Although you want to be thorough during the LOI/due diligence process, you also want to move through this process quickly because it puts an enormous amount of stress on you, your staff, and your company.

When I met with my team at Range, I made sure they understood what my discussions with the buyer were regarding synergies and growth areas. When I work with sellers, I recommend something similar. You want your team to have time with the new buyer so they can present themselves and help show off their talent. You also want to make sure they are viewed as a team and not a disconnected group of employees. It's a good idea to do a mock presentation or interview with your team so each person understands how every other member of that team will answer questions posed by the buyer. This helps the team become more cohesive in their responses, which in turn makes a better impression on the buyer.

### Make Your Company Shine

During this process, your job is to make your company shine. You need your employees to put their best foot forward, so it's critical to touch base with them frequently. I set quick, daily huddles with my I-Team to discuss the status of information that's been sent to the buyer and also to discuss the additional information the buyer has requested. You need to know if any member of your team doesn't agree with your stance on something before that team member meets with the buyer. If the buyer doesn't think you're running a tight ship, the sales process can easily fall apart.

The buyer will have numerous requests about your company that will require your I-Team to step away from their daily roles. If the buyer puts too many demands on one inner circle staff member, decide whether it's worth pushing back. When I sold Range, Deluxe kept asking my marketing person for more and more materials. Finally, I had to step in because that employee was no longer able to do normal duties, which was key to our growth. I asked Deluxe representatives to review our marketing strategy document and write down and send any questions to me prior to the next interview with that staff member. Deciding whether to push back will depend on how critical that particular element is to the sale. If I hadn't sent our marketing strategy through, I would have let Deluxe spend more time with my marketing person.

## Business as Usual

During due diligence, I encourage sellers to run their businesses like they always have. You can't make decisions or changes based on what you think the buyer *might* do because they don't own the company. The only caveat is to consider whether the decision involves long-term commitments such as re-signing a lease or buying a major piece of equipment. If you believe the buyer might want to consolidate space, you might have to think a little harder about this decision.

## The Proof Is in the Pudding

It's critical to remember that due diligence is your chance to prove to the buyer that the claims you made about your company are correct. If you said you have $1 million in inventory, your documents must prove that you have $1 million in inventory. This is the point when the buyer will look through every document you've sent and triple-check that what you've said you have is in fact what you have. In addition to asking for multiple documents from you, the buyer will likely check that you're in good standing with the state, that there aren't any liens against your company, that your taxes are up to date, and that no lawsuits are pending against you.

Close the Deal

## NO REGRETS JOURNAL ENTRY

**PREPARE FOR THE SALES PROCESS.** Map out how your meetings and tours will need to go. What still needs attention? Develop this plan in advance, before emotions consume you.

_____

_____

_____

_____

_____

_____

_____

**CONSIDER LOI/SALE TERMS.** What do you expect or need to know before you would accept an offer? Draft a list now. It will help you build a list of due diligence questions.

_____

_____

_____

_____

_____

_____

**START DUE DILIGENCE.** Who will be on your internal team, or I-Team? What could affect your net proceeds during due diligence? How can you make sure that doesn't happen? Build your own list of due diligence questions. Get your information ready to present before the buyer even has a chance to ask any questions.

_____

_____

_____

_____

_____

_____

_____

_____

_____

_____

_____

_____

_____

_____

# CHAPTER 7

➥

# CLINCH THE CLOSING

*"Always look for the fool in the deal.*
*If you don't find one, it's you."*

— MARK CUBAN

**THE MINUTE SOMEONE HANDS YOU** the pen to ink the signature that will sign your company over to a new buyer, you'll know whether you followed your exit strategy. If you followed it, the backflips in your stomach will be infused with excitement. If you didn't, they'll be fueled by doubt, concern, and possibly regret.

When I sold Alternatives, I felt terrible. I didn't sleep the night before the sale. I woke up at the crack of dawn anxious and apprehensive, and I walked into a high-rise to face my advisor and a table of lawyers and corporate executives. After I signed a ream of papers, I felt like I'd just sold my house without telling my wife and kids. How was I supposed to tell them and my employees that it was over? Alternatives was no longer mine. Unfortunately, because *I didn't know what I was doing going into the sale* and didn't follow an exit strategy, this feeling of dread would only intensify after the sale.

The morning I signed Range over was entirely different. If you remember, the night before the Range sale, I had dinner with the buyers and their team, who asked me numerous times how I felt about things. The morning of the sale, it was just myself and my advisor in the room with one person—who I knew—from the buyer. This person wasn't a stranger. We'd met, we'd eaten together, we had a rapport. He knew how I felt about the sale, and we'd worked closely to develop a deal that worked for both parties.

The atmosphere wasn't tense or impersonal like it was with Alternatives because I was prepared for the sale and the outcome matched my exit strategy. It was actually jovial. We even shared a few laughs about how ridiculous it was that we'd set aside the entire morning to sign a deal we both knew inside and out, and finished within thirty-six minutes. We ended up going to Caribou Coffee to kill time. So instead of feeling alone and full of dread like I did following the Alternatives sale, I had a nice, relaxing morning.

While the aftermath of the Range sale felt better, I want to be clear on one point. No matter who you sell to, you will feel a series of emotions when you sell your company. It's your job to make sure that most of those emotions are positive. For me, the differences between the Alternatives and Range sales were monumental. With Alternatives, I left a corporate tower uncomfortable with my decision, which set the tone for how I felt during the transition period. With Range, I had coffee with someone I enjoyed spending time with. This, too, set a tone for how things went after the sale.

## EXPECT A MOUNTAIN OF LEGAL DOCUMENTS

If you get through due diligence and both parties agree to the sale, expect piles of legal documents that, depending on the type of sale, will include the items listed below:

- Purchase agreement for the business and property/ building
- Flow of funds at closing
- Leases on buildings and/or equipment
- Employment agreements
- Inventory reports
- Contracts for clients, vendors, and financing
- HR materials/handbooks

- Employee lists and noncompetes
- Insurance
- AR/AP
- Open orders
- Process procedure documents
- Debt
- Banks
- Technology information
- Status of business good standing

You will need to read each of these in detail with your attorney, who will help interpret what they mean and help you understand what you're signing. Your attorney should share his or her feelings about the documents with you and your advisor rather than with the buyer directly.

## TRANSITION AND INTEGRATION PLANNING

Whether a transition between ownership is smooth or rocky will have a large effect on how you feel about the sale. Before closing, you need to think about how the buyer will integrate into your company. What's the plan for this? How will you estimate? How will you place orders? How will you bill and collect money? What will these new systems look like and how can you make integration smooth for customers, vendors, and employees?

> **NO REGRETS TIP**
>
> Plan the integration. Whether the transition between ownership is smooth or rocky will have a large effect on how you feel about the sale.

With the Alternatives sale, the transition felt more like the aftershock of an earthquake that we had to react to versus a welcoming transition. I assumed certain things were happening, but I really didn't know what all was needed or was going to happen with our systems or how it would affect our customers. As a result, we ended up spending most our time putting out some massive fires and losing customers.

Before you move to closing, consider how you will develop a smooth transition plan for the following key departments:

### HR

You will need to understand and be able to direct questions about benefits, review processes, hiring/firing and, most importantly, how to collect timesheets and payroll information to the right person. No employees want a surprise on payday!

### Finance

To avoid missing a vendor payment or client invoicing, your accounts payable/receivables and related systems need a transition plan.

### IT

Consider how connectivity to web-based ordering systems will be impacted. Also, consider how your website will connect to the buyer's.

### Operations

Estimating, ordering systems, inventory, and shipping may be impacted by the sale.

### Sales and Marketing

Develop communication plans for broader market announcements, rebrand of collateral, websites, signage, stationery, invoices/statements, marketing campaigns, and connection to your Customer Relationship Management (CRM) system.

Each company will have its own unique transition needs, but it's a good rule of thumb to look through this list and ask which systems within each of your departments might be impacted by the sale.

## PREPARE BEFORE YOU LOSE CONTROL

Understand that your customers will have questions about the change. Develop a script for your employees so they are all sharing the same message with clients. Develop plans for each department, but also define what your goals are and how each fits into the overall plan. Now is the time for planning. If you wait until after the closing documents are signed, it will be too late.

Regardless of how you structure your sale, understand that the minute you sign off on closing documents and receive your check or wired receipt, nothing will be the same for you, your employees, or your customers. You will need to announce the sale and put your transition plan in action. If you're staying on, you'll need to understand your new role in the company, and develop an after-sale planning strategy. You have to understand that the company is no longer yours and do the best you can to ensure that moving forward, things go as smoothly as possible for staff, vendors, and customers.

To minimize the risk, the buyer may withhold a small portion of the payment (5 to 10 percent) for a period of time (six to twelve months) to ensure receivables and reps and warrants are covered. Essentially, the buyer wants to ensure that once they take over, everything the seller stated about the sale—from the condition of the building to the inventory to any pending legal issues—is confirmed.

## DEVELOP YOUR PERSONAL TRANSITION PLAN

After you've developed a transition plan for the company, you also want to develop one for yourself.

Your personal transition plan should be part of your considerations *before* you make the sale. You can tie additional compensation for yourself and the key leaders in your company to your transition plan. This will protect you and your key staff members if the buyer deviates from the agreed plan without your approval.

Before you get started on your plan, remember that it will take time. The earlier you start outlining your plan, the more smoothly the transition will be.

If you sell to a larger company and stay on after the sale, understand that you may not be part of the buyer's leadership team, meaning you will be somewhat in the dark regarding the buyer's plans for you and the company once the sale is complete. If you stay, also understand that you will no longer be allowed to call all the shots. It is important to be clear on this point. Far too many sellers and buyers tell each other that moving forward, it will be business as usual. It won't. You're no longer the owner. You're not responsible for the outcome of all things. Your role in the greater, new company needs to be clear. If it's not in your DNA to take a back seat, you should go the route of transitioning yourself out of the company.

## PLAN YOUR STAFF ANNOUNCEMENT

Your attitude and the amount of time you spend developing your announcement speech and transition plan will greatly affect how things go when you announce the sale to your staff. If you're excited and can clearly answer your employee questions by providing a well-thought-out transition plan that shows who they can report to, you will get a vastly different reaction than if you don't have any clear answers or plan.

Let's look at how this is done poorly and how it's done well.

## ALTERNATIVES STAFF MEETS THE MINNESOTA TIMBERWOLVES

When I owned Alternatives, every quarter I hosted a breakfast meeting at a nearby Radisson hotel for Alternatives employees to talk about the company's performance, growth, progress, and goals. The day of the sale, I met my employees at the Radisson like we did every quarter. When I walked into the conference room, my employees were sitting, facing a large screen, waiting for my normal quarterly business review. I started my presentation a little differently than I had in the past. Instead of showing how we were doing, I talked about the Alternatives journey. I talked about the early days, showed a few pictures with some of the founding team members who all looked younger in out-of-date clothes and hairstyles. That got a few laughs. I showed how the acquisitions we'd made had built a better company by adding more services and allowing us to add the many new team members. When I said this, I purposefully looked at some of the new team members, who smiled back. I then talked about our industry, the changes brought on by the Internet, and new ways to market.

I praised staff for helping us diversify early on, which positioned us to help our clients by providing many new forms of cross-media mar-keting. Then I asked, "So what's next?" and put up a slide that showed a road sign with a fork in the road and text that said, "Which way?" I paused on this slide, which created an uneasy feeling for me. I had a limited plan for delivering the news and thought all was going fairly well so I continued to the next slide, which had a road merging with another lane. It showed the merged lanes going straight ahead. Then I unveiled our new Merrill/Alternatives logo.

On cue, right as I unveiled the logo, the conference room divider opened and a team of what looked like the Minnesota Timberwolves pro basketball team appeared. The new team was very tall—no one was under six feet—and they had another projector ready. It contained a presentation that would give my—now their—confused staff more information about the big surprise. I hadn't reviewed the presentation with them nor did I know how our presentations would or would not complement each other. I thought they would introduce themselves and give a quick overview of their company. Another learning: always review and plan for the buyer's presentation to your employees well in advance of the actual announcement.

## NO REGRETS TIP

Always review and plan for the buyer's presentation to your employees well in advance of the actual announcement.

The buyer's team introduced themselves by talking about the company's accomplishments and financial standing. At the time, they were a public company. Their introduction reflected that. To my *former* staff, the new team and the direction of their conversation was very corporate and somewhat sterile. They seemed unapproachable, which directly contrasted with Alternatives's former high-energy, open culture.

When the president of the division Alternatives fell under finished his overview, he introduced the head of human resources, who began talking benefits. My *former* staff became restless and started talking among themselves. I tried to regain some laughter with a joke about how tall the Merrill team was—the HR woman

Close the Deal

was well over six feet and the department head was 6'7" against my whopping 5'9"—and I got on a chair so I could see eye to eye with all of them. I got a couple of laughs, but it didn't release the tension. The staff had questions they wanted to directly ask me without the new owner or their new boss in the room.

## What About Us?

After a bit, I ended up breaking into the presentation so my staff could ask their questions. They didn't want to hear about growth or transition. They wanted to know about other things, namely, why we were selling and what would happen to their jobs.

The first question was, "Why? Why would you sell the company?"

Whoever asked that question couldn't understand why I'd want to give up eight years of success and growth with an amazing team that had developed an outstanding culture. Trying to answer on the spot and honestly, I thought through my reasons, but found that at that moment—when it was far too late—I really didn't have a good reason for selling.

When I started speaking, I got choked up, grabbed a glass of water, and took a long sip.

It was silent, all eyes were on me, and they all asked, "Why, Paul?"

I told the staff that I truly felt the merger would be best for our clients. I said it would allow us to provide a national platform versus local footprint for them. In addition, we had expanded our product services.

I said, "I believe this will allow us to help deliver more service to our clients so they can grow. If they are more successful, then this provides greater opportunities for all of us as we grow together." My former staff needed to hear this because "clients first" was our rallying call.

However, in the context of that meeting, our rallying call didn't put anyone's mind at ease, mine included.

Somehow, I got through the rest of the questions and breakfast ended with fake smiles and congratulations that I could tell were insincere as the staff huddled in smaller circles discussing the sale. I understood. They wanted to talk among themselves about their futures, but it didn't feel good. I'd never left a company breakfast feeling so hopeless and alone.

## RANGE STAFF MEETS A PARTNER

Telling staff you've sold your company can be difficult because you're telling people you care about—people who have helped you achieve the success that's allowed you to build a business others want to pay for—that you're leaving them. Depending on the deal, you may not leave for a year or five, but you're still leaving the role that has all the control. As a result, everything *will* change.

---

Telling staff you've sold your company can be difficult because you're telling people you care about—people who have helped you achieve the success that's allowed you to build a business others want to pay for—that you're leaving them.

---

However, if you follow your exit strategy, thoroughly plan for your transition, and practice your announcement several times before you make it, which I'll talk about in a minute, you can lessen the pain associated with announcing the sale to staff.

Before the Range sale, I thought about what to say to employees. I tried to anticipate the questions they might ask, and I developed appropriate answers. Because I actually knew why I was selling Range and was confident my reasons for the sale and the deal I brokered fell in line with our exit strategy, I answered the why question confidently and from my heart.

Instead of making the announcement at a third-party location like I did with the Alternatives announcement, I announced the Range sale in our staff room at 3:15 on the afternoon I closed on the sale. I made the announcement like I normally made announcements—between shifts. I did this intentionally. I didn't want anyone learning about the sale from word of mouth, and I wanted to control the message.

## EXPLAIN YOUR WHY

I started the Range announcement by explaining my why. I talked about growth, which was what employees wanted to hear. I then moved into the reason for splitting Range in two. I explained that some staff would move over to Deluxe's management while some would stay under my partner's management. My partner talked about his passion for manufacturing, reiterated his commitment and affection for the third-generation company, and talked about how the sale would help with growth, which would ultimately help all employees.

I then introduced Deluxe as a company without having anyone from Deluxe in the room. I talked about Deluxe and its strategy that I had helped work on all the while returning to my why and reinforcing the fact that the deal would be better for the employees long-term. I explained that representatives from Deluxe would be in the following day to answer additional questions.

Because we were in a familiar environment and the buyer wasn't in the room, the employees were more open with their questions. To get things started, I actually sat next to a few of them and asked questions I would want to know. Unlike the Alternatives sale, Range employees were able to ask questions in a culture they were used to. Therefore, they were more open and willing to talk than they would have been had corporate strangers been staring at them from the front of the room.

After about an hour, things wound down. Staff went home to process the information knowing the Deluxe team would give them more details the following day. My partner and I took our executive team and their spouses out to dinner and gave them bonuses as a thank you for the extra hours they'd put in during the due diligence process.

I can't even remember if I was able to eat dinner the night after the Alternatives sale.

My stomach had been uneasy all day and the last thing I wanted to do following that sale was celebrate. In hindsight, I realize that those feelings were based on the fact that I was starting to understand that I'd made numerous mistakes due to unpreparedness. The dinner following the Range sale, however, was a true celebration. We were all excited. We felt we'd done the right thing for ourselves, our company, and our employees, and had a well-thought-through transition plan to move things smoothly forward. We even received positive feedback from our executive team regarding our employees' thoughts about the sale. Those moving to Deluxe had more questions about the sale, naturally, but the overall feeling was far less contentious than what followed the Alternatives announcement. Following the Alternatives sale, I had an employee come up to me and say, "Paul, how could you do this to us?" It was heart-wrenching.

## PAINT A CLEAR PICTURE

Always prepare for the announcement with staff ahead of time. Put yourself in their shoes and really think about what kinds of questions they'll ask. Anticipate their questions the way you would anticipate questions presented by interviewers for your dream job. They'll want to know:

- Why are you doing this?
- What are you going to do?
- What does this mean to me and my family?
- Will I still have my job?
- Will my pay change?
- Who can fire me or give me a raise?
- What will my benefits look like?

Thinking through how you'll answer these questions gives you an opportunity to paint a clear picture of the future. If you do this well, your staff will understand that you have planned for their future success rather than leaving them. They'll also feel like they're a part of something exciting. This will help address their fears and any remaining will quickly subside.

Prepare for these questions specifically:

### Why are you selling?

Your answer must be strong and from the heart. Explain the thought that went into the sale, how the sale aligns with your exit strategy, and how you plan to take care of employees and clients.

This is a good place to address growth since growth will aid job security, which will help put your employees' minds at ease.

### Why did you pick the buyer?

Your employees are used to working for you and will want to know immediately what the buyer is like. Why did you choose the buyer and why are they good for the company and overall growth? Answering this question is key, particularly if you are not staying during the transition. List the benefits of working for the buyer as they apply to both your employees *and* your clients. Explain that with a new buyer comes more growth opportunities. Introduce the company. Are they a financial buyer that will provide capital for growth, or are they a strategic buyer that has additional capabilities that can leverage your value? Are they a large company or a small company? How will that affect the future for your employees and clients?

### What does this mean to us and our direct reports?

This is a big one. Above anything else, your employees are going to want to know if they have a job. What will happen to them?

While you can't promise what their roles will be—remember, you're no longer the owner, you're acting on behalf of the new owner—share any added benefits. Also, reiterate that if they continue caring for customers, growth and the opportunities associated with it will occur. The buyer wants any company they buy to make sure the existing staff they have are supporting the clients as their main goal.

### What will happen to our clients?

This is where you can introduce your transition plan and explain that during the next few months, each department will work toward a transition that will be seamless for the customers.

### What happens to our company name and brand?

Be prepared to explain that most of the time, the buyer will keep the seller's company name at least for a period of time. They do this so customers don't get lost. Your brand has equity and going from your brand name to an unrecognizable brand may confuse customers. When I sold Alternatives, Alternatives became Merrill Alternatives. When we sold the marketing piece of Range, it became Range, a Deluxe company.

Emotionally, the eventual name change can be tough. Most sellers are really proud of their brand and having it associated with someone else can be difficult. While it's unlikely the name will stay untouched indefinitely, prepare yourself for the change and know that it's coming.

Understand that the announcement will have a deer-in-the-headlights effect on many employees. Know your employees will react differently and respect that. Some may have had an idea that a sale was coming. Others will be totally shocked. Some will be happy for you, some will be mad, and others will be scared because they will be unsure about how it will affect them and their families.

If you don't follow your exit strategy and plan before your announcement, you won't feel good about it. However, if you plan your exit strategy and how you want your announcement to go, it will feel more like a celebration than a loss.

In addition to preparing for the announcement, there are a few other things you can do to minimize the shock. One, if you have employees who will lose their jobs, tell them about it before you make a group announcement. If you do it after the group meeting, you'll lose credibility, and other employees will worry whether they'll be next. During the all-company announcement, state who lost their job and why, and explain that the remaining employees will be part of the go forward plan.

---

> If you have employees who will lose
> their jobs, tell them about it before
> you make a group announcement.

---

When I announced the Range sale, I constantly reiterated this. I knew that if I said it once, some employees wouldn't hear me. I also gave employees a cheat sheet of sorts that answered some of the questions they had about their jobs and the new company. My intent with the sheet was that employees could share it with their family members so everyone was on the same page. I didn't want anything getting lost in translation between the announcement and when employees spoke to their own families.

Close the Deal

## BRIEF CUSTOMERS AND VENDORS

Once you've briefed your employees, it's time to talk to customers. During due diligence, you should review all client contracts. When you get ready to announce the sale, you'll need profiles of each client. These will include a detailed overview of the contract terms and conditions for each client as well as background information about key accounts, average orders, types of projects you do for them, and what to expect from them and when. These profiles will help determine how to announce to each client.

Remember, no one knows your clients and business like you and your team do. These profiles will help determine which clients you, as the previous owner, need to physically announce to, which announcements can be handled by you over the phone, and which announcements can be handled by salespeople, or a letter.

What you don't want to do is send a letter to all your clients or let them find out about the sale from a press release. With the Alternatives sale, I didn't create customer profiles or approach the customers about the sale in person. I didn't know what I was doing so I didn't think to do either.

Immediately, we had calls and complaints from customers who were upset with the new billing system. Because I'd never talked to major customers in person about the benefits of the sale, their first impression of it was negative. When you talk to a client, you get the chance to say, "Hey, this is how this sale will help you." You get to walk them through the transition so they see the benefits that will offset the potential bumps that may occur during the transition.

With Range, I immediately flew out to visit our top clients, called the next tier of customers, and had our salespeople who had better relationships with the third tier of clients call and announce the sale.

Announcing to clients is tough, and you need to be ready for conflicts. Like your employees, your customers are going to want to know right away how the sale will affect them. You need to think like your clients before making the announcement, develop answers to their questions, and practice how you're going to present to each one. Specifically, your clients will want to know how you plan to avoid disruptions to their businesses. The transition plan we outlined earlier in this chapter should answer all their questions about how things will be handled now that ownership has changed.

If there is a conflict with a client, remember that you must support your clients first, even if supporting them differs with the acquiring company's wishes. Generally, if you present the conversation to the buyer in terms of potential revenue loss, the buyer will listen to your thoughts about your client's needs. The buyer will thank you later if you keep the client and their revenue is not lost.

---

## Like your employees, your customers are going to want to know right away how the sale will affect them.

---

Vendors need to be approached in the same way. Think like them, prepare answers to questions they'll ask—namely how the sale will affect them—and sell them on the benefits of the sale. After the Alternatives sale, we lost some vendors who were treated differently after the sale.

Be transparent with your communications to employees, customers, and vendors. Sell them on the benefits of the sale, and tell them exactly how your transition plan will make things as seamless as possible for them.

### BRIEF THE PUBLIC

While the employee, client, and vendor announcements are largely in the seller's control, a public announcement is typically up to the buyer. Sometimes the buyer will go ahead with an announcement; other times, particularly if they don't want competitors to know about the sale, they may keep it quiet.

It's important to note here that your employees, clients, and vendors should know about the sale from you, not a press release. Make sure you talk to the buyer about their plans for announcing so you can ensure employees, clients, and vendors hear the news from you first.

## NO REGRETS TIP
Your employees, clients, and vendors should know about the sale from you.

With the Alternatives sale, some of our clients found out about the sale from the press release. This gave our competitors an advantage. Because we hadn't gone to all our customers and said, "This is happening; here's how it will benefit you," our competitors were able to take some of our clients by saying, "This is terrible for you; come work with us."

## TAKE TIME OUT

There's a period of time between when the announcement is made and new management comes in that you need to use to unwind. Usually, for the month following the sale, nothing will change. Your transition team will begin working through the transition plan and adjusting the timeline as needed. This is your chance to get out of Dodge. Take it!

When we bought Range, we sent the sellers on a cruise so I could lead the company without the emotional impact of them being there. I wanted to get in front and make the changes that needed to be made. When we sold Range, I took time off to recharge and get ready for my reentry as a new employee.

Selling a business is tough. It's emotionally and physically draining, and when it's all said and done, it can be even tougher. If you're staying on, it's tough because you no longer call the shots. If you're leaving, it's tough because that chapter in your life has come to a close. During the days or weeks following the sale, give yourself a break. Take some vacation time and get away. I'm not talking about taking a tour around the world or embarking on your dream vacation. I'm talking about going somewhere that will allow you to reflect on what has happened and what will happen during and after the transition period.

During the break, the buyer will get to know your team better and vice versa while you rewire yourself. If you're staying, you can use this time to accept that things have changed, so when you return to work as a non-owner, you can think of yourself as starting a new job rather than thinking of yourself as an owner who no longer has a company. If you are not staying on, this time will allow you to develop some new routines so when you're no longer showing up to work, you don't feel purposeless.

## NO REGRETS
## JOURNAL ENTRY

**PREPARE FOR CLOSING DAY.** Keep a list of items that were negotiated so you can quickly check them at the closing. Revisit your whys so you are emotionally prepared on closing day, and block off your calendar for the few days following the sale.

_____

_____

_____

_____

_____

_____

**DRAFT AN ANNOUNCEMENT SPEECH.** What will this speech say to meet your whys? Don't wing the announcement. Practice, practice, practice it before making it.

_____

_____

_____

_____

_____

_____

**THINK ABOUT YOUR TRANSITION PLAN.** What part of the plan do you need to be part of? Which part of the plan will you *not* be a part of? What staff changes or introductions must involve you? Set time to remove yourself from the company prior to final duties or your reentry as an employee.

_____

_____

_____

_____

_____

_____

_____

_____

_____

_____

_____

_____

_____

_____

# NO REGRETS

→

*"I have no regrets, because I've always done everything I could to the best of my ability."*

— ROBERT REDFORD

**I KNOW FROM EXPERIENCE** that failing to take the steps to close a sale as outlined in *No Regrets* can lead to long-lasting regrets.

Because I hadn't followed an exit strategy, asked the right questions during my due diligence with Merrill, or developed a strong transition plan, my post-announcement life was a lesson in firefighting.

## FIGHTING THE FIRES

With Alternatives, my first week back after my family trip to California was fairly normal, but Week 2 brought with it a transition manager who had to make sure the two companies would transition without any negative effects on clients and staff.

During that first week back, I learned at a meeting with the buyer's transition manager that we'd be moving from our current IT platform to the buyer's platform. The change offered some positives. We would have better scale, a greater opportunity to grow the business and, in the long term, would save money. However, as I continued asking questions around business needs, especially as it pertained to the client experience, it became clear that there would be some big challenges for clients and employees.

Following that meeting, I met with our sales team and the president of our division to review client contracts. The new president of the division that Alternatives had been rolled into didn't have a sales personality. He was more of a corporate finance guy. There's nothing wrong with that—his style likely worked for his existing employees—but my sales staff was used to a much more robust sales leader and failed to get excited about the many opportunities ahead.

The president of the division talked about the company's plan for growth and how important the Alternatives acquisition was to that growth strategy, which was great. However, he then said, "Going forward, we will need a big bunch of account managers to handle the business, not salespeople."

You could have heard a pin drop after that announcement. The president of the division went on to say that business wouldn't be handled the same, the sales team wouldn't be paid the same way, and the company needed to put more emphasis on the bottom line. Again, this approach may have worked well for others, especially those focused on the bottom line, but my employees were used to something entirely different. They were paid on gross profit that they could control. At that point, many sales staff were whispering to each other and glaring at me wondering, "Why did you do this to us?"

Finally, the transition manager concluded by saying, "HR is coming in to finish the onboarding paperwork. The noncompetes you previously signed have to be re-signed."

In essence, this was a get-out-of-jail-free card for the entire sales team. I was furious *with myself* for not reviewing this in detail before the sale. Incidentally, this began the decline of a once fast-growth company.

When I returned to the office the next week, I noticed the office of one of my top sales reps, who held a large percentage of our revenue, was very clean. As I walked a little farther down the hall, I noticed that another one of our top salespeople had a similarly clean office. When I walked a little further into the conference room, both of the reps were waiting for me with two signed letters that read: "With regrets I am resigning from Alternatives effective today to pursue other interests."

When I asked why they hadn't come to me, they said, "Hey, we trusted you with our noncompete, but now we need to sign a new one with them and we won't do it. We don't have any reason to be loyal to the buyer, we no longer have interest in helping grow this company with new owners, and we are going out on our own now."

I thought about my initial strategy for selling Alternatives, which wasn't thought out and had caused these problems, and wondered how I could get things back on track. With two of my sales staff already leaving to compete against us, I thought, "Okay, I will hire a few new sales recruits and show off the new combined services we offer and find ways to help new customers grow."

Since we had to consolidate our HR and finance functions, I had to set a meeting with the division president to see what process I needed to go through to hire more sales staff and rebuild the lost sales. During that meeting, I learned that we were nearing the end of a quarter and we couldn't add staff at that time.

I was told, "The company is in a hiring freeze. Every dollar saved brings a dollar right to the bottom line, which, with us being public now, has an extremely high multiple or effect on the overall stock price."

I couldn't believe it. Not only had I lost staff, I was also prohibited from hiring new staff members. I failed to understand the possibilities of both prior to the sale.

## EXPECT A CHANGE IN CULTURE

Know that when you sell your company, the fit between your company and the acquiring company needs to be examined *before* the sale. Your culture is what makes your company successful. It's one reason staff decide to work for you over the competition. Understand the impact the acquiring company's culture will have on yours from a negative and positive standpoint. Do they respond slowly? Are they sterile? Are they more conservative? Are they more energetic? Do they have fun and celebrate successes?

The culture at Alternatives was open and built around the idea that success breeds success. Our philosophy was that if we helped our clients be more successful, we would become more successful, which helped us attract more customers and sales talent. Success was part of our culture. We rewarded performance and everyone's compensation was tied to how well we helped our clients. We were able to attract top talent to our company. We received calls from people asking how they could be part of our team. We also received calls from vendors saying they wanted to help us grow. It worked very well. Working for a larger corporation at that time was different.

When I sold Range, I met with other members of Deluxe's staff outside the advisory team to see what they thought the culture was like. If you can, meet with the buyer's staff outside of business hours. They'll be more open to talking and sharing their thoughts on the culture with you.

---

## Meet with other members of the buyer's staff outside the advisory team.

---

Ask the HR team how they approach new hires and how they handle similar issues. Even ask about their dress code. Is it casual or professional? The answers to these questions will help you get a feel for the buyer's culture before the sale.

Understanding the buyer's culture can have a tremendous impact on how your company transitions into the buyer's.

### LIFE AFTER THE SALE

The thing to remember about selling your business is that regardless of whether you stay with the company post-sale, your life will change. Whether that change is positive or negative will largely depend on how well you set yourself up for the sale. Did you follow an exit strategy?

### NEVER BURN A BRIDGE

After the sale of Alternatives, I stayed with Merrill for less than a year, not because Merrill was a bad company—they were a good, growing company that cared for both clients and employees. I left because I had not planned my exit strategy, did not do my proper due diligence, and had not prepared myself for life after the sale. It started with me not understanding the noncompetes and the resigning of the sales staff and continued with the shutting down of Alternatives's fulfillment center. That wasn't something I'd expected or planned for, and it impacted not only how we did business, but also how well we could reach our revenue goals and earnout goals.

Every day I went into the office, it seemed like one thing after another that I hadn't thought about before the sale came up. I felt like someone from the show *The Office*. I'd arrive, punch my timecard, put out fires, and wish away the day until 5 P.M. when I could clock out. This, of course, is not at all how I felt when I owned Alternatives.

A few days after the sale, while I was driving home, I received a call from a large financial investment company. We'd just finished launching the client's web portal and moving their materials into what had been Alternatives's fulfillment center. My client's voice was strained—she was clearly upset—but I didn't know what was going on until she said, "I just learned all of my materials are not going to be filled by your fulfillment center."

Of course, they were going to be filled at the buyer's fulfillment center, but I didn't know that at the time. I was totally shocked. I didn't know what was going on or who had called the client. I asked for a few minutes, hung up, slammed on my brakes, pulled over to the side of the road, and grabbed my notebook. I had to find out who called her and what was going on.

I called our transition manager and left a message. I got through to our account executive and asked if he'd called the client. He hadn't. The transition manager called back and said the request to move materials came from the division president earlier in the week, and the fulfillment manager was then asked to contact the client. When I called the client back, I had to tell her I was doing all I could to stop the move, but when it came down to it, the decision was out of my hands.

The day of the move, my client called again. Her materials weren't at the buyer's fulfillment center, they had been sent to her downtown offices. Not only had we not followed through, we left her with a bunch of materials she needed to get to advisors without any way to get those materials to them.

I called the account executive and asked him to drive down to the client's office immediately to try to help figure out how we could help her get those orders filled. When he arrived, five staff members were sorting through boxes looking for materials. When he tried to help, they turned him away. They said we'd done enough already and sought help from another vendor. I can't express how bad it felt to let down that client because I had not properly planned the sale.

Eventually, the client agreed to let me send some of our former Alternatives fulfillment center staff down to sort out the mess and attempt to save the account. Not long after, I entered a settlement with the buyer regarding a release of my contract. In exchange, I received a reduced earnout amount. I was also released from my five-year employment contract. Despite having been released from my contract, I didn't end on bad terms. In fact, after there was a change in leadership, I ended up going back to work for Merrill for five years as a consultant, which brings up another key point: even if post-sale transitions are not working in your best interest, never burn a bridge. When it comes to business relationships, show respect and conduct yourself as you would have *before* you sold your company. You never know what the future holds.

---

Even if post-sale transitions are not working in your best interest, never burn a bridge. When it comes to business relationships, conduct yourself as you would have *before* you sold your company.

---

Hindsight is a great teacher. Now that more than sixteen years have passed since the sale of Alternatives, I finally know how to complete a no-regrets sale. To complete your no-regrets sale, follow the twenty-two exercises outlined in your *No Regrets Journal.*

# AFTERWORD

➡

*"Hindsight bias makes surprises vanish."*

—DANIEL KAHNEMAN

**NOT LONG AGO, SANDI AND I** took the kids on a trip some might consider insane. All seven of us rented an RV and took a Griswold-style family vacation to South Dakota. We saw the world's largest ball of twine in Dassel, Minnesota; learned how pipes were made in Pipestone, Minnesota; wandered through the Black Hills; and spent a night in a Walmart parking lot. It was a wonderful, easy trip that left us with amazing memories. We checked it off our bucket list as one of our favorites.

On that trip, I reflected to the time following the Alternatives sale when I took a family trip from San Francisco to San Diego. The way I felt on the family trip to South Dakota and the way I felt on the California trip following the sale of Alternatives were worlds apart. Following the Alternatives sale, I couldn't enjoy my time off because I kept reflecting on the things I wished I'd done leading up to the sale. I enjoyed every minute of our South Dakota trip, including staring at the road ahead from our RV, which was a different view than the beautiful

Pacific Coast. I enjoyed it more because my mind was clear. After decades of buying and selling businesses, I knew how to walk away from a sale with no regrets. It's a wonderful, freeing experience.

Of all the lessons I've learned about buying and selling businesses, the one lesson I want to save every business owner from learning firsthand is leaving a sale with regrets. That, in itself, is the reason I wrote *No Regrets*. I've seen far too many sellers—myself included—suffer emotional, physical, and psychological pain because they didn't take the time to *really* think through their sales before putting their businesses on the market.

The minute I started working through the Alternatives sale, I knew I wasn't headed down a good path. I knew it in my heart and felt it in my bones. The closer we got to announcing the sale, the worse those feelings got. During the weeks following the announcement, I couldn't focus. I couldn't turn my eyes away from my employees who were clearly disappointed, or from my customers, who instead of calling to chat, called to unload about their dismay over the changes. Sadly, their complaints were valid, and I knew it. I started taking more headache medication for migraines and dreaded going into the business I had created. It was a terrible experience, one I learned how not to repeat.

The Range sale, of course, was a completely different experience. By following an exit strategy, developing a growth strategy, finding synergies for buyers, vetting buyers, and very clearly defining our transition plans and roles for our employees after the sale, I walked away from that sale without a single regret, emotional or otherwise.

The lessons I learned about selling a business between the Alternatives and the Range sales are what I don't want you to learn firsthand. After you sell your business, I don't want you feeling like you've let everyone down. I don't want you avoiding employees, customers, or vendors because you didn't have enough foresight to really think through the sale. I don't want you feeling good about that large post-sale check one minute only to find yourself scouring the Internet for some new business opportunity the next. I don't want you feeling lost, alone, and full of regrets.

After you close, I want you racing down the highway, the wind in your hair, as you head toward a dinner with your top employees, the buyer, and your family to celebrate the sale. I want to give you the tools I wish someone had given me before I sold Alternatives.

It doesn't matter if you do $200,000 or $200 million in revenue a year. At some point, all of us are going to leave the businesses we created. Maybe we leave it when our time comes, and we have to leave the world we know behind. Maybe we pass it on to a family member. Maybe we close it, or maybe we sell it. Of those exit options, the only one we can control is selling it. You can choose whether to sell your business for the wrong reasons, for the wrong amount, at the wrong time. Or, you can choose the path of no regrets.

If *No Regrets* has done its job, you will understand the planning process for your sale, the steps you'll need to take to close a sale, and the questions you'll need to ask so that when you're ready, you can sell your business without regrets. First and foremost, you should feel comfortable and confident about developing your exit strategy. It will serve as your road map toward your desired exit. Trust that road map. Know that it will lead you to the exit that is the best for you, your employees, your customers, and the buyer.

Next, develop a growth strategy. Complete a SWOT analysis, take a close look at your strengths and weaknesses as well as your competitors and their market share, and create a plan to grow your percentage of that market.

After you've developed those exit and growth strategies and defined your why, what, when, and won't, bring on a phenomenal group of external and internal advisors to help you with the sale, define what you do and do not want from the sale financially and emotionally before you start looking for buyers, understand valuations, and really make an effort to add value to the buyers you're most interested in.

Let your advisors do their magic. Let them negotiate on behalf of that exit strategy so you can keep your emotions out of it. Let them guide you through the steps to closing your sale, but use the information in *No Regrets* to ensure your exit and your outcomes align. Choose an advisor that, more than knowing your industry, is committed to knowing you and what you most want from the sale. Trust that your advisor has your best interests at hand and will work tirelessly to develop a sale that leaves you with no regrets.

If, after working through an exit strategy, you decide that you want to continue with your plan to sell your business and you know a great advisor, that's great. Contact him or her immediately so the advisor can work through every step of the processes outlined in *No Regrets*. However, if you don't know an advisor or don't find yourself connecting to your advisor, Paradise Capital can help. We specialize in helping business owners maximize the financial outcomes from their sale while also minimizing the emotional elements of selling.

I recently worked with a couple who was preparing to shut down and liquidate their twenty-six-year-old family business. Before I talked to them, they thought liquidation was the only way to get out of the business. After speaking with them, I helped them transform their business into a growing, highly sought-after company. They entered into a sale that was right for them and left them with no regrets. Working with businesses owners like this gives me so much joy. I love helping entrepreneurs fulfill their dreams of growing and exiting their business with the best possible outcome.

Whatever outcome you desire for the sale of your business, I sincerely hope the mistakes I learned after selling six of my own companies—several to *Fortune 100* and *Fortune 500* companies—benefits you. If in five years you look back on the sale of your business and the lessons you've learned in *No Regrets* and say, "I'm so glad I did," rather than, "I wish I would have," then I've done my job.

# 22 JOURNAL ACTIONS FOR A NO-REGRETS SALE

## CONSOLIDATE YOUR CHAPTER NOTES BELOW OR USE THIS FOR YOUR ANNUAL PLANNING

1. **Start your exit strategy now**. Don't wait until someone approaches you about selling and it's too late. Journal your why, what, when, and won't below.

\
\
\
\
\

2. **Complete your baseline valuation and compile a list of key performance indicators (KPIs)**. What do you need to track as part of your exit journey so, going forward, you can track your results/progress to see where you need to make adjustments?

\
\
\
\
\
\

3. **List what you are doing well today.** What do clients appreciate most about working with your company? What else can you do for them? Writing this list will help you avoid a knee-jerk reaction (selling too early) to short-term challenges. For a free exit strategy questionnaire, visit www.paradisecapital.biz.

_____

_____

_____

_____

4. **List which market or markets you're currently in.** Now, list the market or markets you should be in.

_____

_____

_____

_____

5. **List your available market size.** What percent of this market do you have and what are your goals for capturing more of this market?

_____

_____

_____

_____

_____

6. **Complete a SWOT analysis.** What growth-related actions do you need to take to get to your goal?

_____

_____

_____

_____

_____

7. **Commit to a marketing campaign.** What will it look like? How will you stick to it? How will you measure it?

_____

_____

_____

_____

8. **What does your ideal sale look like?** Write what your best sale would look like. What would the buyer look like? How will you feel? How will your employees feel? Who are the key employees you want to protect post-sale? What will the culture be? What will you net from the sale? What do you see yourself doing after the sale?

_____

_____

_____

_____

_____

9. **What does your worst sale look like?** What would the buyer look like? How will you and your employees feel following that sale? What would you net from that sale? What can you do now to prevent this scenario? How will you adjust your exit strategy to prevent this from happening?

_____

_____

_____

_____

10. **What does a good day versus a bad day at your company look like?** What makes a day good or bad? Do they stay the same or change? What can you do so you don't leave during a bad day or bad year filled with regrets?

_____

_____

_____

_____

11. **Choose your A-Team.** Who do you have already? Who do you need to meet?

_____

_____

_____

_____

12. **Choose a baseline valuation method.** Either choose one from *No Regrets* or use one you have been using already, but make sure you use the same one year over year. Journal the results and annually compare them to your exit strategy and "what" goal.

_____

_____

_____

_____

13. **Examine your documents.** Which ones don't you have? Which ones need to be clarified or produced? Develop a process to keep your files in order so they are ready to present to a buyer.

_____

_____

_____

_____

14. **Build your prospect list.** Who would be your dream buyer? Complete a company spoon test and refine this list annually.

_____

_____

_____

_____

15. **Start thinking about your marketing teaser.** What are your company's strengths today? What would catch a buyer's eye? Do this year over year. Do your answers change? Do you need to do things differently from year to year to attract the right buyer?

---

---

---

---

16. **Think about your company's accomplishments.** Which accomplishments would you list for your company if you were building a resume for it? What do you need to adjust, build, or buy to improve your company?

---

---

---

---

17. **Prepare for the sales process.** Map out how your meetings and tours will need to go. What still needs attention? Develop this plan in advance, before emotions consume you.

---

---

---

---

18. **Consider LOI/sale terms.** What do you expect or need to know before you would accept an offer? Draft a list now. It will help you build a list of due diligence questions.

_____

_____

_____

_____

19. **Start due diligence.** Who will be on your internal team, or I-Team? What could affect your net proceeds during due diligence? How can you make sure that doesn't happen? Build your own list of due diligence questions. Get your information ready to present before the buyer even has a chance to ask any questions.

_____

_____

_____

_____

20. **Prepare for closing day.** Keep a list of items that were negotiated so you can quickly check them at the closing. Revisit your whys so you are emotionally prepared on closing day, and block off your calendar for the few days following the sale.

_____

_____

_____

_____

21. **Draft an announcement speech.** What will this speech say to meet your whys? Don't wing the announcement. Practice, practice, practice it before making it.

_____

_____

_____

_____

22. **Think about your transition plan.** What part of the plan do you need to be part of? Which part of the plan will you *not* be a part of? What staff changes or introductions must involve you? Set time to remove yourself from the company prior to final duties or your reentry as an employee.

_____

_____

_____

_____

**For a free downloadable *No Regrets* 22 Journal Actions, visit www.paradisecapital.biz**

# ABOUT THE AUTHOR

After building six companies and selling numerous companies to *Fortune 100* and *Fortune 500* companies, Paul Niccum has faced the same fears and emotional concerns that all sellers face. As both a seller and a buyer—Paul has also acquired eight businesses during his career—Paul is passionate about sharing with other business owners the lessons he's learned about growing and exiting businesses. Of the hundreds of lessons Paul's learned, he is adamant about teaching sellers how to properly sell their businesses so they don't walk away with emotional regrets.

Today, Paul mentors business owners through his company, Paradise Capital, to maximize the financial rewards of their sales while also helping them reduce the negative emotional side effects of those sales. Paradise Capital works with companies that are in the midst of all facets of the merger–acquisition process to make sure the sellers meet their goals when selling their business.

Paul lives on a lake in Northern Minnesota with his wife, Sandi. Both Niccums are avid outdoor enthusiasts who love the water. They spend time boating, waterskiing, wake boarding, surfing, paddle boarding, and enjoying Minnesota's beautiful landscape. They also like to travel and have stayed everywhere from Walmart parking lots in Sioux Falls, South Dakota, to thatched huts in Bora Bora.

The Niccum family just welcomed their first granddaughter, Briella, whom they all adore, to the family.

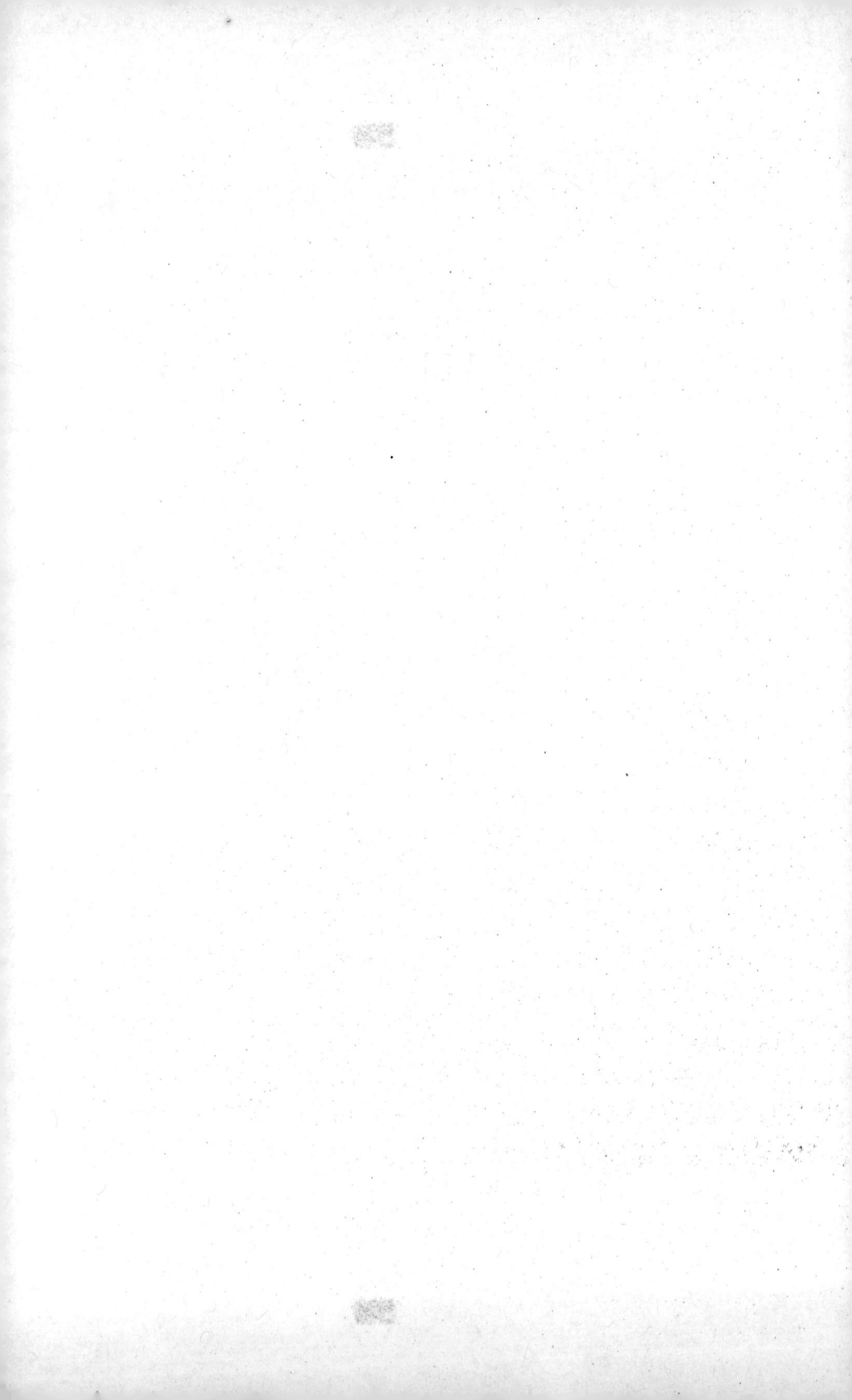

# RECOMMENDED READING

*The Entrepreneur Roller Coaster*, Darren Hardy

*They Can't Eat You*, Marc Sparks

*Challenge to Succeed*, Jim Rohn

*Good Leaders Ask Great Questions*, John Maxwell

*Innovator's Dilemma*, Clayton Christensen

*Seeing What's Next*, Clayton Christensen and Scott Anthony

*Selling at Mach 1*, Steve Sullivan

# PARADISE CAPITAL

## ARE YOU READY?

PHONE: (612) 670-6773

EMAIL: info@paradisecapital.biz

www.paradisecapital.biz